THE NORTH END

Italian Cookbook

"Buonopane has a number of secrets that make her recipes unique."
— *The Boston Globe*

"Marguerite's ravioli is so well known in this historically Italian neighborhood of Boston that the recipe itself has become something of a culinary celebrity."
— *Yankee* magazine

"Not your ordinary pasta compilation . . . [this] cookbook provides a gastronomic gold mine of over 150 original Buonopane family recipes. . . . She brings the tastes of the Old World to the New, never losing her family's Northern Italian heritage."
— *Boston Woman*

"I found it near impossible to read Buonopane's recipes without getting hungry. . . . No Italian kitchen, or any kitchen, should be allowed to continue pretending to be purveyors of delectable meals without the presence of Buonopane's cookbook, at least kitchens where cooks intend to be successful."
— *Post-Gazette,* Boston

"Buonopane has won a culinary reputation that has grown beyond her Italian-American neighborhood. . . . [She] has concentrated on her favorite dishes plus selections from family and friends. One thing hasn't changed. The book remains Italian-American to the core."
— Copley News Syndicate

THE NORTH END
Italian Cookbook

Third Edition

by Marguerite DiMino Buonopane

Chester, Connecticut

Acknowledgments

Ma, thank you for everything you taught me. Your patience and love are what I hope to reflect in this book, along with your wonderful cooking.

Angelo, my darling husband, thank you for sharing me with the mounds of notes and recipes scattered all over the house while I was preparing this book.

Many thanks to my brother, Dom, and my sister-in-law, Toni-Lee, for your unlimited expertise in preparing good food and your generosity in sharing it with us.

Thank you to my son Sal, my mother-in-law, Ann, my friends Patty, Claire, and Nancy, and our seniors Maria, Fanny, Lucy, Margaret, Rose, Suzy, and my dearest Savina.

Bob O'Brien, your moral support, encouragement, and willingness to help kept me going. Thank you for assisting me with such cheerfulness and good spirits. I never could have done it without you!

The photographs in this book, taken by Ben Lipson, capture the flavor of one of America's most extraordinary communities — Boston's North End.

Library of Congress Cataloging–in–Publication Data

Buonopane, Marguerite DiMino.
    The North End Italian cookbook/Marguerite DiMino Buonopane.
    — 3rd ed.
    p.   cm.
    Rev. ed. of: North End Union Italian cookbook.
    Includes index.
    ISBN 0-87106-159-7
    1. Cookery, Italian.   I. Buonopane, Marguerite DiMino. North End
    Union Italian cookbook.   II. Title.
    TX723.B785   1991
    641.5945—dc20   91-15919
                                                        CIP
Manufactured in the United States of America
Third Edition/First Printing

Contents

▌▌▌▌▌▌▌

Papà

Introduction

IIIIIII

I love to cook. That's partly because I love to eat. I also love
the smells of garlic and oil that fill my kitchen when I
cook, and I love the way my Italian neighborhood of Boston's North End smells. The restaurants in the neighborhood send their perfumes of sauces and Marsala floating
through our streets, and I am completely lifted from all
matters except wanting to run home to cook and eat!

Even when I was growing up, the wonderful smells of
Italian cooking were special to me. My mother's cooking
filled the air with aromas that made us happy to come
home each day. Because of my mother, our family kitchen
was the focal point of our home in the North End of Boston. It was the area where we all gathered and shared so
many good moments. We cooked, ate, played games, did
our homework, and sat and talked in this one room.

Today, I feel very close to my mother when I cook. I try
to recapture every step she so carefully took with even the
simplest meal—so careful that the food almost kissed us
while we were eating. And that's what it was meant to be—
love, hugs, and kisses from a tired woman who worked
hard to provide us with all the comforts she possibly could.

During my childhood, I was always happy to have my
mother cook for me, but I never wanted to learn how to
cook, and I never wanted to help her cook. I can still pic-
ture how I sat at the kitchen table, doing my homework
and hoping my mother would not notice me and ask me
for help. Little did I know that I was learning how to cook
Italian through my subconscious. There is a routine to Italian cooking, a repetition of one form or another, as most
recipes use tomatoes, olive oil, chopped garlic, grated
cheese, chopped parsley, and so on. Everything my mother
did stayed in the back of my mind, so when I was first
married and had to cook a meal, I was able to put all the
steps together and prepare a good Italian meal! I have loved
to cook ever since.

My love of cooking led to my coordinating the first *North
End Italian Cookbook*. About thirteen years ago, when I
started working at the North End Union, fund raising was an

important need. Our first cookbook developed from the Italian senior citizens—mothers and grandmothers—who met at least twice weekly at the Union. They had much knowledge of Italian cooking that had never been captured on paper, and they were willing to share their old family recipes in the *North End Italian Cookbook*. As the coordinator of the book, I was asked to be on television and radio shows, and then to teach cooking classes and run a luncheon at the Union every week as a fund raiser. All these activities led to my writing this second *North End Italian Cookbook*, which is a collection of my own favorite recipes, plus ones from a few friends and family members.

I hope the recipes in this book will serve as a guideline to help you learn Italian cooking. Many of the recipes I am including are old family recipes, cooked in the way I remember my mother and grandparents used to cook. I call it peasant style, as our family recipes are from the Roman region of Italy, where they were the foods of the common people. Because there are many different ways to prepare Italian food, it is important for you to realize that you can incorporate many different styles of cooking and perhaps bring together a style of your own—one that suits your family's tastes. Please don't get discouraged by the many ingredients used in some of the recipes. Try to improvise and use what you have on hand. Add a little more or a little less of this or that ingredient and make cooking fun. By experimentation and improvisation, many cooks have become great. With this cookbook, you too can become a great cook, pleasing your friends and family with the wonderful aromas and delicious tastes of Italian cooking.

Antipasto, Salads, and Appetizers

||||||||

Antipasto Salad Platter

IIIIIII

I serve antipasto as a way of keeping my guests happily eating while I'm in the kitchen putting the finishing touches on the other courses. The salad dressing is also good on any garden salad. It will keep indefinitely in the refrigerator.

> *1 head romaine or iceberg lettuce, washed and*
> *   drained*
> *1 red bell pepper, thinly sliced*
> *1 green bell pepper, thinly sliced*
> *4 large mushrooms, wiped clean and sliced*
> *¹⁄₄ pound Provolone cheese, thinly sliced*
> *1 8-ounce can chickpeas, drained*
> *¹⁄₄ pound Genoa salami, thinly sliced*
> *¹⁄₂ cup small black pitted olives*
> *1 large tomato, cut in wedges*
> *1 medium onion, thinly sliced*

1. Trim the lettuce and tear the leaves into bite-size pieces. Arrange the leaves on a large serving platter.
2. Add the remaining ingredients, spreading them evenly over the lettuce.

Salad Dressing

IIIIIII

> *¹⁄₂ cup olive or vegetable oil*
> *¹⁄₄ cup lemon juice*
> *1 teaspoon salt*
> *¹⁄₂ teaspoon freshly ground black pepper*
> *¹⁄₈ teaspoon dried crushed red pepper flakes*
> *1 garlic clove, crushed*
> *1 tablespoon snipped fresh basil leaves, or 1*
> *   teaspoon dried basil*

1. Combine the ingredients in a jar with a tightly fitting lid. Shake until well blended.
2. Pour the dressing onto the antipasto ingredients and toss gently, using two large spoons. Serve.

Serves 8

Arugula and Radicchio Salad

IIIIIIII

Salad

2 bunches arugula
2 small heads radicchio

1. Rinse and trim the arugula.
2. Cut the cores from the radicchio, rinse, and tear the leaves into bite-size pieces.
3. Dry arugula and radicchio. Wrap in paper towels, place in a plastic bag, and refrigerate until cold, about 30 minutes.

Creamy Garlic Dressing

$^1/_2$ large egg yolk
juice of $^1/_2$ lemon
1 tablespoon red-wine vinegar, plus additional to taste
1$^1/_2$ teaspoons mustard (Dijon), plus additional to taste
1 clove garlic, minced
salt and freshly ground pepper to taste
$^1/_4$ cup olive oil
2 tablespoons vegetable oil
2 tablespoons chopped fresh parsley

1. Whisk the egg yolk, lemon juice, vinegar, mustard, garlic, salt, and pepper.
2. Gently mix in the oils until the mixture forms a creamy consistency.

3. Just before serving, place the greens in one or two large salad bowls. Divide the dressing evenly between the bowls. Toss well to combine. Garnish with parsley.

Serves 6

Tomatoes with Fresh Basil and Olive Oil

▌▌▌▌▌▌

1 pound yellow, orange, or red plum tomatoes
 OR cherry tomatoes (whatever is in season
 or readily available)
¼ cup fruity olive oil
10–15 fresh basil leaves
salt and freshly ground pepper to taste

1. Place the tomatoes in a colander; rinse well under cold running water. Drain and pat thoroughly dry with paper toweling.
2. Toss the tomatoes with the olive oil, basil leaves, and salt and pepper to taste in a medium bowl.
3. Let stand at room temperature until serving time, tossing occasionally. This makes a nice appetizer or side dish.

   NOTE: This recipe can also be prepared with regular-size fresh ripe tomatoes, sliced. Simply brush the slices with a little olive oil and sprinkle with salt, pepper, and the basil leaves. Add some pitted, dry-cured black olives for garnish.

Serves 3–4

Pignoli, Tomato, and Fresh Basil Salad

||||||||

2 tablespoons pignoli (pine nuts)
4 large ripe tomatoes
2–3 bunches medium-size basil leaves
dressing (recipe below)
salt and freshly ground pepper to taste

1. In a small frying pan, using medium heat, stir the pignoli until the nuts are lightly browned, about 5 minutes. Set aside.
2. Core the tomatoes and cut them crosswise into ¼-inch slices. Arrange the tomato slices and basil leaves equally on each of four salad plates.
3. Spoon the dressing over the vegetables and garnish with the pignoli nuts. Season to taste with salt and pepper. Serve at room temperature or cold.

Dressing

In a bowl, whisk together ¼ cup dry white wine, 2 tablespoons each minced shallots, chopped fresh basil leaves, and lemon juice, and ¼ teaspoon freshly ground pepper.

Yield: 4 individual servings

Green Bean and Potato Salad

||||||||

This recipe makes a delicious warm or cold salad. Serve it for lunch with leftovers or as a side dish at dinner.

1 pound fresh green beans, tips removed, and
*   snapped in half*
½ pound small potatoes, unpeeled
⅓ cup olive oil

3 tablespoons wine vinegar
2–3 garlic cloves, chopped
1 tablespoon dried oregano
1 tablespoon chopped fresh parsley
pinch dried red pepper flakes (optional)
salt and freshly ground black pepper to taste

1. Cook the beans in 2 quarts of salted water for 8 to 10 minutes, until tender. Drain and place on a serving platter.
2. Boil the potatoes until tender. Drain (do not rinse), let cool, and then cube, leaving the skin on. Add to the green beans.
3. Using a large spoon, gently toss the beans and potatoes with the remaining ingredients.
4. Serve the salad at room temperature or refrigerate for a marinated flavor.

Serves 4–6

Lentil Salad

IIIIIIII

3 cups lentils, picked over, washed, and drained
¹⁄₃ cup red-wine vinegar
¹⁄₂ cup olive oil
¹⁄₄ cup finely chopped red onion
¹⁄₂ cup finely chopped scallions (white part only)
2 tablespoons chopped fresh mint
2 tablespoons chopped fresh parsley
salt and freshly ground black pepper to taste

1. Bring a large saucepan of water to boil. Drop in the lentils and return the water to a boil, stirring often. Lower the heat and let the lentils simmer steadily for 18 minutes or until they are tender.
2. Drain them into a colander, shake to remove excess moisture, and pile into a bowl.
3. While still hot, add the vinegar and oil and stir gently but thoroughly. Let them sit until they cool completely.

4. Add the onion, scallions, mint, parsley, salt, and pepper; stir again.
5. Cover with plastic wrap and leave at room temperature for 2 hours for the flavors to mellow, stirring occasionally.
6. Taste for seasoning and serve at room temperature.

Serves 6

Insalata di Fagioli

IIIIIIII
Bean Salad, Italian Style

This makes a wonderful appetizer because you may add lots of interesting ingredients that will add to the color.

*1 20-ounce can cannellini beans, rinsed and
    drained well
2 tablespoons lemon juice
olive oil
salt and freshly ground pepper to taste
1/4 cup chopped fresh parsley
2 cloves garlic, chopped
black dry-cured olives (optional)
red pepper, chopped into bits (optional)*

1. Place the beans in a serving dish large enough to accommodate the beans neatly.
2. Toss them gently with fresh lemon juice, olive oil, salt and pepper, fresh parsley, and chopped garlic.
3. Garnish with black olives, which have been pitted and cut in half, and red pepper for crunch and color. Serve at room temperature.

    NOTE: I like to add strips of red roasted peppers, canned or fresh, for added color.

Serves 4

White Kidney Bean Salad

▌▌▌▌▌▌▌

*2 cans (1 pound each) white kidney or cannellini
   beans, drained, rinsed, and drained again
1 cup coarsely chopped celery, including the leafy
   top from 1 rib
1 small red onion, halved lengthwise, then cut into
   thin vertical slices
½ cup olive oil
¼ cup lemon juice
1 teaspoon salt
¼ teaspoon freshly ground pepper
10 pitted, dry-cured olives (optional)*

1. In a large bowl, combine all the ingredients; toss lightly.
2. Let stand at room temperature at least 30 minutes for
   flavors to mellow, or cover and refrigerate overnight. If
   refrigerated, bring to room temperature before serving.

Serves 4–6

*Melanzana con
Olio e Aceto*

▌▌▌▌▌▌▌

Pickled Eggplant

*salt
1½ pounds eggplant, sliced very thin
3 cloves garlic, cut into large pieces
2 basil leaves, chopped fine OR ½ teaspoon
   dried basil
½ teaspoon oregano
1–2 hot green peppers (optional)
1½ cups wine vinegar
oil*

1. Sprinkle salt very lightly on the sliced eggplant. Let stand about 30 minutes.
2. Put the slices into a pile and press until most of the liquid drains out. Squeeze well and wipe dry.
3. Arrange the slices in a 1-quart screw-cap jar that has been sterilized.
4. Add the garlic, basil, oregano, peppers, and vinegar to every other layer until all ingredients are used. Press down firmly and pour enough olive oil to cover the eggplant mixture.
5. Store in refrigerator at least 48 hours. Serve as an appetizer with crackers or toasted French bread.

Yield: 1 quart

Marinated Mozzarella

||||||||

*3 packages (5 ounces each) mozzarella
  string cheese*
4 large cloves garlic, peeled
*2 medium bell peppers (preferably 1 red and 1
  green), diced*
1 small onion, sliced thin
*2 1/2 teaspoons dried basil leaves, crumbled, mixed
  with 1/4 teaspoon crushed red pepper*
2 tablespoons vinegared capers, drained
2 tablespoons red-wine vinegar
1 1/2 cups olive oil

1. Cut the mozzarella sticks in 3/4-inch pieces. Thread two toothpicks or wooden skewers with 2 garlic cloves each; place in clean 1-quart jar.
2. In layers, add half the mozzarella, bell peppers, onion, basil/red pepper mixture, and capers; repeat layers. Then add vinegar and oil.
3. Cover and refrigerate; let steep for 2 weeks before serving.

   NOTE: This makes a great gift when you tie a seasonal ribbon around the neck of the jar and attach a label with serving suggestions.

Serves 4-6 as appetizer

Mom's Potato and Egg Frittata

IIIIIII

A frittata is an Italian peasant version of the French omelette. It is used to turn eggs into a full meal.

> *8 large eggs*
> *3 tablespoons milk*
> *¹/₄ cup freshly grated Parmesan cheese*
> *2 tablespoons chopped fresh parsley*
> *salt and pepper to taste*
> *¹/₄ cup plus 1 tablespoon olive oil*
> *2 medium potatoes peeled and thinly sliced*
> *1 medium onion, thinly sliced*

1. In a large mixing bowl, beat the eggs with a whisk or fork until foamy. Add the milk, grated cheese, parsley, salt, and pepper.
2. Heat ¹/₄ cup of oil in a heavy skillet over high heat. Sprinkle a dash of salt on the bottom of the pan and add the sliced potatoes (the salt will prevent potatoes from sticking). Fry about 5 minutes or until crisp.
3. Add the sliced onions and cook until tender, tossing gently with a spatula.
4. Put the potato and onion mixture in the bowl of beaten eggs. Stir gently.
5. Return the skillet to the heat. Drizzle in the tablespoon of olive oil to coat the pan sides, using a rotating motion. Pour the egg mixture into the pan, reduce the heat to medium-low, and stir briskly with a fork, pulling the cooked egg from the sides to the center of the pan. Continue stirring until the mixture starts to set. Cook slowly until the edges start to brown.
6. Remove the frittata from the heat, cover, and let rest for 5 minutes. Cut into wedges and serve.
7. If you prefer to brown both sides of the frittata, place a large plate on top of the skillet and slide the frittata out. Then, flip it upside down back into the skillet so that the uncooked side is down. Cook for 5 minutes more. Remove from the heat and let rest 5 minutes.

Serves 6

Hot and Spicy Omelette

IIIIIII

6 eggs
2 tablespoons warm water
1/4 cup freshly grated Parmesan cheese
2 tablespoons chopped fresh parsley
salt and pepper to taste
1/3 cup olive oil
1 medium onion, thinly sliced
1/4 pound sliced mushrooms
3 large hot vinegar peppers, sliced
2 tablespoons grated mozzarella cheese
6 pitted black olives, halved
2 ounces canned roasted peppers, cut in pieces
pinch of fresh basil or mint

1. In a large mixing bowl, whisk the eggs until foamy. Add the water, grated cheese, parsley, salt, and pepper.
2. Heat the oil in a large skillet over medium heat. Add the onions, mushrooms, vinegar peppers, and a shake of salt and pepper. Saute.
3. When the vegetables are tender, raise the heat to high. When the pan is hot, slowly drizzle the egg mixture over the vegetables in the pan, gently pushing the edges of the batter to the middle of the pan where it is the hottest. This will enable the omelette to set properly.
4. When the omelette is three-fourths firm, sprinkle with the mozzarella cheese, olives, roasted peppers, and pinch of basil or mint. Cook a few more minutes.
5. Turn off the heat, cover the pan and let the omelette set for 5 to 7 minutes, or until it is moist and firm. Cut into wedges and serve immediately.

Serves 4

Onion Omelette

IIIIIII

¹/₃ cup olive oil
1 large red or white onion, peeled and cut into
  rings
6 eggs
2 tablespoons water
1 tablespoon chopped fresh parsley
¹/₄ cup freshly grated Parmesan cheese
salt and freshly ground black pepper to taste

1. Heat the oil in a large heavy skillet over medium heat until it is fairly hot but not burning.
2. Add the onion rings to the skillet and reduce the heat to medium-low. Cook the onions until limp, about 10 minutes, stirring often. Using a slotted spoon, transfer the onions to a plate.
3. In a medium-size bowl, beat the eggs, water, parsley, grated cheese, salt, and pepper.
4. Return the skillet to high heat. When it is hot, but not burning, lower the heat to medium and slowly pour in the beaten eggs. Lift the edges slightly so that the uncooked portion runs to the bottom. Continue to lift the edges until the omelette is almost firm.
5. When the bottom is golden brown, add the onions. Fold the omelette in half and turn it onto a platter. Serve immediately.
6. If a pielike omelette is desired, reduce the heat to low after the onions have been added, cover, and let set for 5 to 10 minutes. You may also flip over the omelette and brown the other side, as described for the Potato and Egg Frittata. Slide onto a large platter, cut into wedges, and serve immediately.

Serves 3

Prosciutto and Melon

||||||||

This recipe makes an excellent, light, and tasty appetizer. If you like a decorative look, serve it on a bed of lettuce with a few black olives on the side. The color combination is very attractive!

> *1 large cantaloupe or honeydew melon*
> *8 ounces imported prosciutto, thinly sliced*
> *1 lime, cut in 8 wedges*

1. Cut the melon into 8 wedges. Remove the seeds from each wedge, but leave on the skin.
2. Make crosswise cuts ¹/₂ inch apart into each wedge, cutting down close to the skin. Lay the wedges on serving plates or a serving platter.
3. Drape a piece of prosciutto across the top of each wedge of melon. Top with a lime wedge.
4. To eat, squeeze the lime onto the prosciutto. Cut into the prosciutto where the melon has been cut, and then lift up a piece of melon and prosciutto on your fork.

Serves 8

Soups

Old-Fashioned Chicken Broth

||||||||

This broth is a good do-ahead recipe, as it should be refrigerated for a day before using it to let the fat congeal so it can be discarded. This broth also freezes perfectly.

> 1 3½-pound fowl, quartered
> 2 tablespoons salt
> 1 tablespoon black pepper
> 4 medium carrots, scraped and sliced
> 3 celery stalks with leaves, chopped
> 4 fresh parsley sprigs
> 4 small potatoes, peeled
> 3 fresh tomatoes, chopped, or 1 cup canned
>   tomatoes
> 2 large onions, quartered
> about 10 tablespoons freshly grated Parmesan or
>   Romano cheese

1. Wash the fowl thoroughly and remove and discard excess fat. Place the fowl in a large stockpot and add the vegetables and seasonings. Add cold water to 1 inch above the height of the ingredients.
2. Bring the pot to a gentle boil, then reduce to a simmer. Cook slowly, uncovered, for about 2 hours. (The fowl may be removed after 1½ hours if it is cooked through, but the stock should continue cooking for another half hour.) Reserve the fowl.
3. Cool the broth and then refrigerate. The next day, remove and discard the congealed fat from the top of the broth. Remove the vegetables. You may push them through a food mill back into the broth to produce a thick, hearty broth. I like to cut up the vegetables into the broth or place a few pieces of cut-up vegetables on top of each serving of broth. The chicken may be served as a side dish to the broth or boned and put into the broth.

4. Reheat the broth and serve with about a tablespoon of grated cheese on each serving.

VARIATION: Just before serving, add 2 cups of cooked rice to the strained broth and heat until the rice is hot. Or cook ¹/₂ pound tiny pasta such as *acini di pepe* in 2 quarts boiling water, drain, add to the strained broth, and serve immediately. Note: If pasta remains in the soup for a period of time, it will absorb much of the broth and thicken it. Only add pasta when the broth is ready to serve.

Serves 10 (generously)

Chicken Soup with Escarole and Polpettini

IIIIIIII

Once you accomplish making a homemade soup, it will become a simple and enjoyable task. The secret to this task is the secret to all Italian cooking—having the basic ingredients on hand. That will always encourage you to plunge into almost any recipe without fear.

> *1 plump fowl, about 4–5 pounds*
> *2 celery stalks with leaves, halved*
> *2 fresh parsley sprigs*
> *2 scraped carrots*
> *1 large ripe tomato, chopped*
> *salt and pepper to taste*
> *1¹/₂ pounds escarole, well washed and cut*
>   *crosswise into thin shreds*
> *¹/₂ cup water*
> *1 pound ground beef*
> *2 tablespoons freshly grated Romano cheese*
> *1 teaspoon chopped fresh parsley*
> *¹/₂ pound tiny pasta such as pastina, orzo, or*
>   *acini di pepe*

1. Clean and wash fowl well. Discard excess fat. Place fowl in a soup pot and add cold water to cover. Bring it slowly to a boil and skim the surface often.
2. When the water stays fairly clean, add the celery, parsley, carrots, tomato, salt, and pepper.
3. Cover the pot tightly and cook slowly over low heat until the fowl is tender, about 2½ hours. Strain the broth. (The chicken may be used for chicken salad sandwiches another day or the white meat may be boned and added to the broth.) Refrigerate the broth until the fat has congealed on top. Remove and discard the fat.
4. Reheat the broth over medium heat. Put the escarole in a large skillet with the ½ cup water. Simmer for 3 minutes, strain, squeeze out excess water, and add to the broth.
5. Combine the ground beef, cheese, parsley, and salt and pepper to taste. Shape into balls no larger than a filbert (dip hands in water to keep the balls smooth and round), and drop into the hot, semi-boiling soup. These are the *polpettini* (tiny meatballs).
6. Cook the soup for ½ hour on low heat to combine the flavors thoroughly and to cook the meat.
7. Cook the pasta in 2 quarts of boiling salted water. Drain, do not rinse, and add to the soup just before serving.

NOTE: This soup can be refrigerated for several days. It also freezes well.

Serves 10–15

IIII Since I work during the week, Saturday has become my day to prepare some of the ingredients needed for the week's menus. I find that it saves me a lot of time during the week when I prepare chopped parsley and garlic, grated cheese, and bread crumbs in advance. They can be put in plastic bags and stored in the refrigerator for at least one week. IIII

Stracciatella Soup

||||||||

This is a quick soup that looks elegant on the table but takes very little work in the kitchen. It will keep in the refrigerator for at least 3 days, and it freezes well.

> *2 eggs*
> *¹/₈ teaspoon salt*
> *freshly grated Parmesan cheese*
> *1 quart homemade chicken broth (see page 12), or canned*
> *chopped fresh parsley for garnish*

1. Combine the eggs, salt, 2 tablespoons of cheese, and 3 tablespoons cool broth in a mixing bowl. Beat with a wire whisk for about 3 minutes.
2. Bring the remaining broth to the boiling point. Add the egg mixture slowly, stirring constantly with a fork. Let the soup simmer for at least 5 minutes.
3. Pour the soup into individual bowls and sprinkle with parsley and more grated cheese, if desired.

Serves 4

Nonna's Beef Soup

||||||||

> *1 to 2 beef soup marrow bones, with marrow, cracked*
> *1 pound beef chuck or eye of round*
> *3 fresh tomatoes, chopped, or 1 8-ounce can tomatoes, squeezed to break into small pieces*
> *2 carrots, scraped*
> *1 large onion, quartered*
> *1 potato, peeled*
> *3 celery stalks with leaves, halved*
> *3 parsley sprigs*

salt and pepper to taste
1/2 pound pastina or acini di pepe, cooked and
drained just before soup is ready to serve
freshly grated Parmesan cheese for garnish

1. Place the soup bones in cold water and boil for 3 minutes. Drain and rinse well.
2. Place the washed bones, beef, vegetables, and seasonings in a large soup pot. Cover with cold water, two inches above the ingredients. Slowly bring to a gentle boil, removing any foam that may form on top.
3. Simmer, covered, for about 2 1/2 to 3 hours, stirring from time to time. Remove bones, meat, and vegetables. Shred the beef and reserve. The vegetables may be served as a side dish to this soup.
4. Strain the broth into another large pot and return to the heat. Add the cooked pasta and shredded beef. Pour into individual soup bowls and sprinkle with grated Parmesan cheese.

   NOTE: This soup freezes well or can be refrigerated for at least 3 or 4 days.

Serves 6

My Homemade Minestrone Soup

I concocted this recipe at a North End Union luncheon, using the leftovers of the previous day. You might find it a good way to use yours. Garlic bread makes an excellent accompaniment.

1 quart cold water
1 medium onion, chopped
1 8-ounce can whole green beans, undrained
1 8-ounce can chickpeas, undrained
1 8-ounce can red kidney beans, undrained

1 small zucchini, unpeeled and diced
1 celery stalk with leaves, chopped
2 carrots, peeled and thinly sliced
1 16-ounce can chicken broth or 2 cups
homemade broth
1 medium cabbage, chopped (remove center core)
1 8-ounce can medium-size peas, undrained
Quick Pesto Sauce (see recipe below) (optional)
1 8-ounce can tomato sauce or 1 cup Marinara
Sauce (see page 30)
1/2 cup uncooked pastina, tubetini, acini di pepe,
or raw rice
salt and pepper to taste
freshly grated Parmesan or Romano cheese

1. Place the first 11 ingredients in a large pot and bring to a slow boil. Lower heat and simmer uncovered for 1 1/2 or 2 hours, stirring often.
2. Add the pesto sauce and tomato sauce to the soup. Taste for more seasonings.
3. Ladle the soup into bowls and sprinkle with grated cheese.

Serves 6–8

Quick Pesto Sauce

1/4 cup olive oil
1 garlic clove, chopped
1 tablespoon chopped fresh basil leaves
1 tablespoon chopped fresh parsley
1/2 cup freshly grated Parmesan or Romano cheese

1. Blend the ingredients in the blender until smooth.

IIII Prepare garlic ahead of time by peeling and chopping it, and then storing it in a small jar or plastic bag. Refrigerate up to a week, if you wish. The chopped garlic will be very handy to throw into a frying pan with some olive oil and parsley for a quick garlic sauce, or for any other use you wish. **IIII**

La Minestra Mom's Way

||||||||

This recipe reflects a truly "old style." It takes a while to prepare, but it is very nourishing and flavorful. It should be started the day before you wish to serve it. See your butcher for a fresh prosciutto bone. Don't concern yourself with its size, but have the butcher cut it into small pieces.

1 cup white navy or pea beans
1 fresh prosciutto bone with meat attached
¹/₂ pound pepperoni, cut in chunks, OR 2 pounds
spareribs, boiled, drained, and rinsed well, OR
2 pigs' feet, boiled, drained, rinsed well
7–8 garlic cloves, crushed
1 large Savoy cabbage, outer leaves removed,
quartered
¹/₂ cup olive oil
salt and pepper to taste
dried red pepper flakes for garnish

1. Wash the beans well, removing any imperfect ones. Soak overnight.
2. Soak the prosciutto bone for 6 to 8 hours in a bowl of water in the refrigerator, changing the water often.
3. Boil 6 cups of water. Gradually add the beans to the boiling water. Simmer 2 minutes, and remove from heat. Set aside to soak for 1 hour. Then rinse beans and strain.
4. Boil the prosciutto bone and the meat of your choice for 20 minutes. Rinse and strain. This will remove any fat or residue.
5. Put the clean prosciutto bones, your chosen meat, and the prepared beans in a large heavy pot. Cover with cold water to an inch over the bone and beans. Add 3 cloves of garlic. When the water comes to a boil, lower the heat and simmer. When the prosciutto meat starts to pull away from the bone (about 30 minutes), shut off the heat. Separate the meat from the prosciutto bones and put the meat back in the pot.

6. In a separate large pot, cook the cabbage until tender. Do not overcook. Strain, reserving some of the liquid. Put the cabbage in the pot with the beans and prosciutto.
7. Fry 4 or 5 cloves of garlic in the ½ cup of olive oil until brown. Add to the cabbage and beans. If the sauce seems too thick for your taste, add some of the cabbage broth. Simmer the entire mixture for 5 minutes, stirring with a wooden spoon. Add salt and pepper to taste (be careful with the salt, as prosciutto and pepperoni are highly salted).
8. Remove the pan from the heat and let rest for at least 2 hours so that all the flavors will be well combined. Refrigerate until ready to serve.
9. When you are ready to serve, reheat *La Minestra* on a low burner, heating only as much soup as needed. Serve in large bowls, topped with red pepper flakes. It is excellent with crusty Italian round bread.

Serves 6–8

Pasta e Fagioli

IIIIIIII

Pasta and Beans

This soup can be used as a lunch dish or as a first course at dinner.

To Prepare Beans

½ pound white navy or pea beans
6 cups cold water (sometimes I use leftover or
*   canned chicken broth for a richer flavor)*
¼ cup olive oil
2 garlic cloves, crushed
salt and pepper to taste

1. Wash the beans thoroughly and discard any imperfect ones.
2. Put the cold water in a large pot. Add the beans, garlic, oil, salt, and pepper.
3. Simmer until the beans are tender, about 1 ½ hours.

Marinara Sauce

1 garlic clove, chopped
pinch of dried red pepper flakes, basil, mint, and oregano
3 tablespoons olive oil
1 8-ounce can tomatoes
salt and pepper to taste

1. In a small heavy skillet, slowly saute the garlic and seasonings in the olive oil on low heat until golden brown.
2. Add the tomatoes and a pinch more of each of the seasonings. Add salt and pepper to taste.
3. Simmer, uncovered, for 10 minutes on low heat.

To Finish Soup

1 teaspoon salt
2 quarts water
½ pound ditali, *small shells, or elbow macaroni*
freshly grated Parmesan cheese

1. Put the salt in the water and heat to boiling in a large saucepan.
2. Gradually add the pasta. Boil rapidly, uncovered, about 12 minutes or until *al dente*. Reserving 1 cup of liquid, drain the pasta in a colander, rinsing under cold water to prevent sticking. Reserve.
3. When the beans are tender, add the drained pasta and the marinara sauce to the pot. If more broth is desired, add the 1 cup of liquid from the pasta. Simmer 10 to 15 minutes.
4. Ladle into large soup dishes and sprinkle with grated Parmesan cheese. Serve immediately or the pasta will swell and absorb all the soup.

Serves 4–6

Pasta e Piselli

IIIIIII

Pasta and Peas

This makes a tasty and nourishing lunch, especially with garlic bread.

> *¹/₄ cup olive oil*
> *1 small onion, chopped*
> *1 large garlic clove, chopped*
> *2 teaspoons tomato paste*
> *1 14-ounce can peeled Italian plum tomatoes*
> *pinch of dried basil, mint, and red pepper flakes*
> *1 8-ounce can medium-size sweet peas*
> *salt and freshly ground black pepper to taste*
> *1 pound small shells, ditali, or elbow macaroni*
> *freshly grated Parmesan or Romano cheese for*
>   *garnish*

1. Heat the olive oil in a heavy saucepan, and saute the onion and garlic. When transparent, add the tomato paste. Mix well.
2. Add the canned tomatoes and juices, squeezing the tomatoes to break them up. Saute for a minute or two, then add basil, mint, and red pepper flakes. Stir gently for about 3 minutes over medium-low heat. Add the undrained can of peas. Simmer the sauce while you cook the pasta, adding more seasonings if desired and salt and pepper to taste.
4. Meanwhile, bring 4 quarts of salted water to a boil. Add the pasta. Boil rapidly, uncovered, about 10 minutes or until tender. Drain in a colander, reserving 2 cups of the water. Do not rinse. Transfer the pasta back to the pot, and add the tomato sauce and peas mixture.
5. Stir gently and add the pasta water until the sauce produces a nice broth texture. Remember that this is in the soup family.
6. Serve immediately with plenty of grated cheese.

Serves 6–8

Italian-Style Split Pea Soup

IIIIIII

This is great for lunch or as a first course, especially with a ham dinner. It can be refrigerated for several days or frozen.

> *1 1/2 cups green split peas, picked over, washed,*
>   *and drained*
> *1 large onion, chopped*
> *2 celery stalks, chopped*
> *1 large leek, chopped*
> *1 large garlic clove, halved*
> *1 large ripe tomato, chopped*
> *1 large carrot, peeled and chopped*
> *3 quarts cold water*
> *1/4 cup olive oil*
> *salt and pepper to taste*

1. Place the peas in a 4-quart stockpot with the vegetables and the cold water. Drizzle with the olive oil.
2. Let the stock come to a boil. Stir well and add salt and pepper. Simmer for about 1 hour, or until the peas are cooked tender but not mushy.
3. Ladle into large soup bowls and serve with croutons or garlic bread.

Serves 6–8

IIII A good way to begin preparing a recipe is to always have the basic ingredients on hand. The basics for Italian cooking are usually tomatoes—canned and/or fresh—fresh garlic, fresh parsley, freshly grated Italian cheese (Romano or Parmesan), fresh bread crumbs, and good olive oil. IIII

Lentil Soup

IIIIIII

Even if you do not like lentils, you will not be able to resist this soup. My daughter used to turn up her nose at lentil soup when she was young. Now, as a married woman, she keeps containers of it in the freezer to serve to her friends gathered around the fireplace on a cold winter night. And she doesn't hesitate to accept the rave reviews!

> *¹/₂ pound lentils, picked over, washed, and*
> *   drained*
> *1¹/₂ quarts cold water*
> *2 or 3 celery stalks with leaves, finely chopped*
> *2 small carrots, chopped*
> *1 tablespoon chopped fresh parsley*
> *1 onion, chopped*
> *1 garlic clove, chopped*
> *1 tablespoon olive oil*
> *3 ripe tomatoes, peeled and chopped, or ¹/₂ cup*
> *   canned tomatoes*
> *salt and pepper to taste*
> *¹/₂ pound ditali, small shells, or elbow macaroni*
> *freshly grated Parmesan cheese*

1. Place the lentils in a large pot with the cold water. When the water comes to a soft boil, add the remaining ingredients, except the pasta and grated cheese.
2. Simmer, covered, for ¹/₂ hour or more, until tender.
3. Meanwhile, cook the pasta in 2 quarts of salted water until *al dente*. Drain the pasta, reserving 1 cup of liquid. Add the pasta to the soup.
4. Taste for seasonings and simmer 5 minutes. If the soup seems too dry, add some or all of the reserved pasta water.
5. Ladle into large soup bowls, sprinkle with grated cheese, and serve immediately for lunch or dinner along with a garden salad or antipasto.

   NOTE: This soup freezes well or can be refrigerated for several days.

Serves 4–6

Mediterranean Three-Bean Soup

||||||||

1/3 cup olive oil
2 leeks, coarsely chopped
2 stalks celery, coarsely chopped
2 cloves garlic, minced
4 cups chicken broth, fresh or canned
1 teaspoon thyme
1 teaspoon marjoram
1 bay leaf
pepper to taste
1 1/2 cups cooked kidney beans
1 1/2 cups cooked garbanzo beans
1 pound string beans, cut into 1-inch pieces
grated cheese

1. Heat the oil over moderate heat in a large soup pot.
2. Add the leeks, celery, and garlic and saute 3 to 4 minutes. Add the remaining ingredients except for the string beans and grated cheese.
3. Bring the soup to a boil; then lower heat. Simmer for 20 minutes.
4. Add the string beans and simmer for 15 to 20 minutes more, until the string beans are cooked but still crunchy. Serve with grated cheese.

Serves 4

Sauces and Gravies
||||||||

Marinara Sauce

The difference between plain meatless tomato sauce and marinara is texture and color. Tomato sauce is prepared with tomato paste, giving it a darker, richer body and flavor. Marinara sauce is light, almost pinkish, and can be cooked in 10 or 20 minutes for a delicate effect. It also can be frozen. Use it over cooked thin spaghetti or linguine.

1/2 cup olive oil
2 garlic cloves, chopped
1 teaspoon dried red pepper flakes
1 teaspoon dried basil
1 teaspoon dried mint
1/4 teaspoon dried oregano
1 28-ounce can crushed or whole plum tomatoes,
 with juice, or 12 peeled fresh tomatoes
salt and pepper to taste, plus pinch more of above
 seasonings
1 tablespoon chopped fresh parsley

1. In a large heavy skillet, on low heat, very slowly heat the oil, garlic, and the red pepper flakes, basil, mint, and oregano. Let cook for about 5 minutes or until the garlic is golden brown.
2. Raise the heat to medium-high. When the oil is really hot, add the tomatoes. (If you are using the plum or fresh tomatoes, crush them in your hands or put them in a blender for 1 second before adding them to the pan. This will speed up the cooking process and give a smoother consistency to the sauce.) Let the sauce come to a soft boil.
3. Add salt and pepper to taste, and a pinch more of red pepper, basil, mint, and oregano. Add the chopped parsley. Let the sauce simmer, uncovered, for about 15 minutes, stirring occasionally with a wooden spoon.

VARIATIONS: This is a wonderful sauce to use as the basis of other recipes. Add a can of clams, or sliced mushrooms, or sliced black olives. Be inventive! I gradually add the juices from the canned clams or mushrooms to the sauce as well, until I produce the texture my family enjoys. Other additions might include a can of crabmeat or a pound of cut-up baby squid or lobster meat.

Yield: 4 cups

Sunday Gravy

IIIIIIII

This tomato sauce with meat is called gravy because the meat drippings become the base for the sauce. It is meant to feed the whole family abundantly. You may cook up to 3 pounds of pasta and have enough sauce and meat to make everyone happy. It refrigerates and freezes well. You may use any or all of the meats listed.

> *1 pound sweet Italian sausages*
> *2 pounds meatballs (page 94)*
> *4–5 lean pork chops*
> *1 pound lean spareribs*
> *1 pound piece of beef or pork*
> *¹/₂ cup olive oil*
> *1 medium onion, chopped*
> *1 garlic clove, chopped*
> *pinch of dried basil, red pepper flakes, oregano,*
>   *and mint*
> *1 6-ounce can tomato paste*
> *1 28-ounce can peeled and crushed tomatoes*
> *1 28-ounce can water*
> *salt and pepper to taste*

1. Fry the meats of your choice in ¹/₄ cup of the oil in a large heavy saucepan.
2. When they are browned, transfer them to a platter. Add the remaining ¹/₄ cup of oil to the residual juices in the pan. When the oil is hot, saute the onion, garlic, and seasonings until transparent.
3. Stir in the tomato paste and blend well. Add the tomatoes and stir until blended with the tomato paste and

oil. Stir in an extra pinch of the seasonings. Add water, using the 28-ounce can from the tomatoes. (Keep adding water until the sauce remains the thickness you desire. I use a full can.)

4. Let the sauce come to a full boil and add salt and pepper to taste and an additional pinch of herbs. Return the meat to the pan. Then simmer over medium heat, uncovered, for at least 1 hour or until all of the meat is fully cooked. Stir gently every 15 minutes or so, using a large wooden spoon.

5. Serve the sauce over pasta, reserving some additional sauce for individual servings at the table.

NOTE: Pork added to the gravy will make an oily— though delicious—gravy. When you are using a significant amount of pork, skim the excess oils off of the top of the sauce. Pork also tends to produce a thin sauce, so go easy when adding additional water, or add an extra can of paste at the beginning of the preparations. This will help maintain the body of the sauce.

Serves 10–12 generously

Tomato Gravy with Ground Meat

IIIIIII

This sauce uses tomato paste, which produces a heavier texture than that of the Quick Meat Sauce recipe.

> *¹/₂ cup olive oil*
> *1 medium onion, chopped*
> *1 large garlic clove, chopped*
> *1 pound lean ground beef (or ¹/₂ pound ground beef and ¹/₂ pound ground pork)*
> *1 6-ounce can tomato paste*
> *salt and pepper to taste*
> *1 28-ounce can peeled and crushed or Italian plum tomatoes*
> *1 teaspoon dried basil*

1 teaspoon dried mint
1 teaspoon chopped fresh parsley (optional)
¹/₄ teaspoon dried red pepper flakes (I use a little more)
¹/₄ teaspoon dried oregano
1 tomato-paste can water

1. Heat the olive oil in an enamel or stainless steel heavy saucepan. Add the onion, garlic, and the ground meat. Stir with a wooden spoon and work it over well to break up any possible chunks of meat.
2. When the meat is browned and sort of crusty, but not burned, add the tomato paste. Blend well and sprinkle in a little salt and pepper.
3. Add the tomatoes and blend well. (If you are using the plum tomatoes, put them through a sieve or in a blender to crush them.) Sprinkle in the seasonings and more salt and pepper. Stir well. Simmer, uncovered, for at least 20 minutes on low heat, stirring occasionally and gently with a wooden spoon. After 10 minutes of simmering, pour in the can of water until you reach the consistency you desire.
4. Serve the sauce over pasta, eggplant, lasagne, or manicotti.

Yield: approximately 6 cups

Quick Meat Sauce

||||||||

The total cooking time for this sauce is approximately ¹/₂ hour, and it can be cooked ahead and reserved. It refrigerates well for several days and freezes excellently.

¹/₄ cup olive oil
1 pound ground meat (¹/₂ pound beef, ¹/₂ pound pork)
1 small onion, chopped
1 garlic clove, chopped

pinch of dried basil, red pepper flakes, and mint
salt and pepper to taste
1 28-ounce can peeled and crushed tomatoes

1. Heat the oil in a large skillet. When it is rippling hot, add the ground meat and start to brown it, stirring with a wooden spoon. When partly browned, add the onion, garlic, and seasonings. Continue browning until the meat is a little crisp on the bottom of the pan.
2. Add the can of tomatoes and mix until the sauce starts bubbling. At this point lower the heat and add additional salt and pepper to taste, stirring well. If the mixture is too thick, add some warm water to smooth it a bit.
3. Sprinkle in an additional pinch of basil, red pepper flakes, and mint. Let the sauce simmer, uncovered, on low heat for about 20 minutes, and stir it often.
4. Serve over a pound of cooked pasta, or use as a topping for eggplant, lasagne, manicotti, ravioli, or stuffed peppers.

Yield: approximately 6 cups

Cooked Fresh Tomato Sauce

IIIIIIII

The difference in this sauce is its sweet, fresh taste. The recipe makes enough sauce to coat at least 1 to 1½ pounds of any bought or homemade pasta. If you desire to add some fish or meat to the sauce, you may do so immediately after the sauce is prepared and just keep cooking until the fish or meat is cooked.

12 ripe tomatoes
½ cup olive or vegetable oil
1 carrot, scraped and chopped
1 small celery stalk with leaves, chopped

1 medium onion, chopped
1 garlic clove, chopped
pinch of dried basil, mint, and red pepper flakes
salt, freshly ground black pepper

1. To blanch the tomatoes, put them into boiling water for a couple of minutes. After the skin begins to shrink from the fruit, remove them from the water and run under cold water to finish the process of peeling.
2. After the tomatoes are peeled, put them in a pot with no water. Let them boil until they are cooked, about 10 minutes. Then mash or blend them in a blender until they have the consistency of a cooked sauce. Now they are ready for use.
3. Heat the oil in a large heavy saucepan. Add the carrot, celery, onion, garlic, and a pinch of basil, mint, and red pepper flakes. Saute until the vegetables are tender, but not burned.
4. Pour in the tomatoes and mix well. Let the sauce come to a soft boil. At this point you can determine if you wish to add some water. You also can add salt and pepper and additional basil, red pepper, or mint.
5. Stir for a couple of minutes, lower the heat, and let simmer for 1/2 hour or more, stirring often, but gently, with a wooden spoon. I like the oils to accumulate on top of the sauce at this point because I feel they seal in all the flavors. So I stir very gently, trying to scrape the bottom of the pan without disturbing the accumulation of oils.
6. Add meatballs, ground meat, or fish, if you choose, and cook until they are cooked through. Serve over pasta.

Yield: approximately 6 cups

Uncooked Fresh Tomato Sauce

||||||||

This is a different and exciting way to use your fresh garden tomatoes. Serve on linguine or thin spaghetti as a main dish with a barbecue of meat, fish, or chicken.

> *1 pound red ripe plum tomatoes*
> *1 garlic clove*
> *1 shallot clove*
> *4 fresh basil leaves*
> *salt and pepper to taste*
> *$1/4$ teaspoon dried red pepper flakes*
> *$1/2$ cup olive oil*

1. Peel the tomatoes and remove the hard stem. Cut into small cubes and remove seeds (squeeze with hands). Place in a blender or a food processor with the garlic, shallot, basil, salt, black and red pepper, and olive oil. Blend at high speed for one or two seconds, or until the tomatoes are somewhat crushed and combined with the other ingredients. Do not overblend. Serve at room temperature.
2. This makes enough sauce for $1/2$ pound pasta. Sliced black olives and chopped parsley make a nice garnish for the dish. The sauce is also good as a pizza sauce.

Yield: approximately 2 cups

|||| Italians tend to lean toward fresh foods in cooking. Fresh tomatoes, when available, are a must for most sauces. Fresh garlic, fresh parsley and basil, freshly grated Italian cheese, and fresh bread crumbs are also necessary. All of these are a big help in making a good meal better! ||||

Aglio e Olio

||||||||

Garlic and Oil Sauce

This sauce is delicious on spaghetti (about ³/₄ pound is the right amount). If you like garlic, you would also like this sauce with shrimp, as shrimp scampi, or as a sauce with clams, Linguine Vongole.

> *1 cup olive oil*
> *5 garlic cloves, chopped*
> *¹/₂ teaspoon freshly ground black pepper*
> *¹/₄ teaspoon dried red pepper flakes (optional)*
> *1 tablespoon chopped fresh parsley*
> *1 tablespoon chopped fresh basil (optional)*

1. Heat the oil until warm. Add the garlic and simmer slowly for about 5 minutes or until the garlic is golden. Do not burn. You may remove the garlic at this point or leave it in if you enjoy a strong garlic flavor.
2. Add the black and red pepper, parsley, and basil. Stir well and use as desired.

Yield: 1 cup

Red Clam Sauce

||||||||

This sauce is delicious over pasta (about ¹/₄ pound), used as a topping for pizza, or served as a broth with whole clams in shells.

> *10 littleneck clams, in shell*
> *approximately 4 cups heated marinara sauce (see*
> *   page 30 or use your favorite recipe)*
> *2 tablespoons dry white wine*
> *chopped fresh parsley*
> *salt and freshly ground black pepper to taste*

1. Scrub the clams thoroughly with a clean brush. Rinse under cool running water.
2. Put the clams in a pot with the marinara sauce and wine. Cover. Let the clams steam for about 5 to 7 minutes, or until they open. Remove the clams as soon as they have opened, to prevent toughness.
3. Add parsley and salt and pepper to taste.
4. If you serve this sauce with pasta, toss the noodles with about 4 tablespoons of butter to keep them from absorbing too much of the sauce. Arrange the clams in their shells on the sides of the platter of pasta. Sprinkle the pasta with grated Parmesan or Romano cheese.

Yield: approximately 4 cups

Pesto Sauce

IIIIIII

This excellent recipe for pesto came from Dom's Restaurant. This sauce is served uncooked, at room temperature, over cooked pasta. It makes an elegant dish when used with tortellini, fettuccine, and other favorites. It is also excellent when added to minestrone or pasta *primavera*. When all the ingredients are on hand, the sauce takes about 5 minutes to prepare. It also can be refrigerated or frozen indefinitely for future use; just warm it up at room temperature.

> *2 cups olive oil*
> *2 firmly packed cups whole fresh basil leaves*
> *2 cups fresh parsley leaves*
> *4 garlic cloves*
> *¹/₂ cup pignoli (pine nuts)*
> *1 tablespoon freshly ground black pepper*
> *1 teaspoon salt*
> *1 cup freshly grated* Pecorino *or Romano cheese*
> *¹/₂ cup water*

1. Put all the ingredients except the basil into a blender and grind thoroughly. Then add the basil and grind until a creamy texture is achieved. No cooking is needed.
2. This amount of sauce is enough for 1 pound of pasta of your choice.

Yield: 2 pints

Alternative Sauces for Fresh Pasta

▌▌▌▌▌▌▌

Spinach Sauce

¼ cup butter or margarine
1 10-ounce package frozen chopped spinach
1 teaspoon salt
1 cup ricotta cheese
¼ cup grated Parmesan cheese
¼ cup milk
⅛ teaspoon ground nutmeg

1. In a 2-quart saucepan over medium heat, in hot butter, cook spinach and salt 10 minutes.
2. Reduce heat to low; add remaining ingredients. Mix sauce well and cook until just heated through (do not boil).

Yield: 2½ cups

Walnut Sauce

¼ cup butter or margarine
1 cup coarsely chopped walnuts
½ cup milk
2 tablespoons minced parsley
1 teaspoon salt

1. In a 9-inch skillet over medium heat, in hot butter, lightly brown walnuts (about 5 minutes), stirring occasionally.
2. Stir in remaining ingredients; heat.

Yield: 1⅓ cups

Pasta and Bread

||||||||

Some Tips on Cooking and Serving Pasta

▌▌▌▌▌▌▌

Since all pasta is cooked the same way, it is not necessary to repeat the cooking directions for each dish. However, here are a few general pointers so that your pasta will not be cold and gummy before the sauce is done.

Store-bought pasta will take about 10 to 15 minutes to cook; homemade or fresh pasta from the delicacy shop only takes about 3 or 4 minutes. These cooking times are measured from the time the cooking water returns to a full boil after the pasta is added.

There should be plenty of water in the cooking pot to allow the pasta to float around easily and uncrowded. Always have the cooking water rapidly boiling when you first put the pasta into it, and softly boiling as the pasta is cooking. Don't start cooking the pasta until your sauce is ready, or the ingredients for the sauce are fully ready.

After the pasta has been cooked and sauced, it should be served immediately. Don't let it stand at room temperature; don't even try to keep it warm or hot in the oven while you eat your appetizer. The pasta should be served as soon as it is prepared. The only exception would a *primavera*, which keeps well and therefore can be made in advance.

A true Italian serves the pasta as the first or main course, with the meat and salad coming after it.

Ravioli

▌▌▌▌▌▌▌

Because this recipe can be somewhat tedious, I suggest you invite a friend over to prepare it with you. That way you can share both the work and the rewards. If you make the ravioli one day and freeze them, and the sauce another day and freeze it, you'll be putting together your meal without a lot of last-minute fuss. To make the ravioli, you will need a lightly floured, flat, unpainted surface; I use my kitchen counter or an old table without any veneer. A heavy rolling pin on ball bearings will make the dough much easier to roll out. Don't get discouraged! It will take you a few times to get comfortable with making ravioli.

Basic Ravioli Dough

*6 cups unsifted unbleached flour (King Arthur
    preferred)*
3 eggs
1 teaspoon salt
boiling hot water (about ¾ cup)

1. Pour the flour on your preparation surface and form a well in the center. Add the salt to the well. Add the eggs to the well, breaking them gently with your fingers. Mix the flour and eggs together until they form a cornmeal texture.
2. Make another well and gradually add hot water, constantly shifting the flour on top of the water (so you won't burn your hands), until you are able to handle the mixture. The dough should be soft and pliable. If you find it too moist, add more flour to the working surface and knead the dough directly on top of it. If the dough is too dry, keep wetting your hands with warm water as you work the dough until it handles well.
3. The dough should be kneaded for about 8 minutes or until it becomes smooth enough to roll. A thorough kneading mixes the ingredients and develops elasticity in the dough. Knead dough by folding the opposite side toward you. Using the heel of your hand, gently push the dough down and away from you. With your fingertips, squeeze it and push it back to you. Fold the dough over envelope-style, and repeat the process over and over. When the dough has been kneaded enough, its surface will feel satiny and will look smooth. For a beginner, this might take 10 to 12 minutes, while an experienced person may need 5 to 8 minutes. Throughout this process, use as little additional flour as possible.
4. Place the kneaded dough in a bowl, pat it with some water, and cover with a clean cotton cloth or an in-

verted bowl to prevent drying. Let it rest for 30 minutes before attempting to roll it out. Remember, the dough should be very smooth in order to work well. While the dough is resting, you can make the filling.

NOTE: Many people feel that they should add at least a half dozen eggs to this recipe, because that's what Grandma used to do. That is fine, but it should be remembered that the resting period for a dough with more eggs must be longer—at least an hour. Working people without much time should keep this in mind. A dough with many eggs that is not sufficiently rested will simply "bounce back" in the rolling process. To be blunt, it will go nowhere.

Ravioli Filling

2 pounds ricotta cheese
3 medium eggs
2 additional egg yolks
1/2 cup freshly grated Parmesan or Romano cheese
1 garlic clove, pressed
1/2 cup chopped fresh parsley
salt and pepper to taste

1. Mix the ingredients thoroughly in a large, wide bowl. Reserve.

To Finish Preparation

*1 recipe Tomato Gravy with Ground Meat (see
    page 32)*
*1 pound, approximately, grated Parmesan or
    Romano cheese (freshly grated preferable)*

1. Divide the dough in half, keeping the other half covered with an inverted bowl. Roll out the dough on a lightly floured surface until it is about 1/8 inch thick. Repeat with the second half.
2. Drop teaspoonfuls of filling about 2 inches apart on one sheet of dough until the filling is used. Cover with the other sheet.

3. With your fingertips, gently press around each mound of filling to form a little filled round. Cut apart into 2-inch squares with a pastry cutter or a special ravioli cutter (available at a specialty shop in all sizes and shapes). Make sure the edges are well sealed. Sprinkle the finished ravioli with a little flour and let rest until the water is boiling.
4. Meanwhile, bring approximately 8 quarts of salted water to a boil in a large pot.
5. Using a spatula, gently lift the ravioli into the rapidly boiling water. The ravioli will keep rising to the top of the water during cooking, crowding each other. Lower the heat to medium and gently press the ravioli back down into the water, using a large, flat, slotted soup skimmer. This step is important because it allows the ravioli to cook evenly. Continue for at least 10 minutes.
6. Taste to see if dough is tender enough to serve. (I always wait for the pasta to cool before sampling; somehow it changes its texture after it is out of the water.)
7. Strain gently and thoroughly, one third at a time, and place on a large serving platter. Form three layers of ravioli, gravy, and grated cheese. Continue until all the ravioli is on the platter, ending with gravy and grated cheese.

NOTE: Ravioli can be made earlier in the day it will be served; just sprinkle with flour and cover with a dry cloth. Ravioli can also be frozen in the following manner: Place a few pieces at a time on a cookie sheet and place in the freezer. When they are frozen, place them in a plastic freezer bag. Continue this process until all the ravioli are frozen. They will keep indefinitely in this way. When ready to use, gently drop into boiling water as you would the fresh product.

Yield: 5–6 dozen

Manicotti

IIIIIIII

Stuffed Pasta

If you have ever eaten manicotti made with the store-bought pasta, you should be sure to try this recipe. There's no comparison. Homemade manicotti is much lighter and fluffier.

> *Basic Ravioli Dough (page 43)*
> *vegetable oil*
> *2 pounds ricotta cheese*
> *2 pounds spinach, boiled, drained, squeezed dry, and chopped*
> *4 large egg yolks*
> *2¹/₂–3 cups freshly grated Parmesan cheese*
> *1 large garlic clove, pressed*
> *¹/₄ cup chopped fresh parsley (reserve 2 tablespoons for topping)*
> *salt and pepper to taste*
> *¹/₂ recipe Tomato Gravy with Ground Meat (page 32)*

1. Follow the ravioli dough recipe until the rolling-out stage. Then, divide the dough in half and roll it on a lightly floured surface until it is paper thin. Cut into 5 x 6-inch rectangles. Continue until all the dough is used up.
2. Cook the pasta rectangles in 8 quarts of boiling salted water in a large pot. Add a drizzle of oil to prevent the pasta from sticking together. Cook about 12 to 15 minutes or until tender, stirring often with a wooden spoon. Rinse well under cold water, but be careful to prevent the pasta from tearing. Drain well and reserve while you make the filling. Run the noodles under cold water occasionally and loosen them with your hands until you are ready to use them.
3. Mix together the ricotta, spinach, egg yolks, 1 cup of grated cheese, garlic, parsley, salt, and pepper.

4. Spread 2 tablespoons of the mixture on each piece of cut pasta. Roll envelope-style, carefully tucking all ends together halfway through the roll to prevent the filling from oozing out.
5. Place the filled manicotti side by side in a baking pan with the tucked ends on the bottom of the pan. Cover the manicotti with a layer of gravy and grated cheese. Sprinkle with the 2 tablespoons of reserved parsley.
6. Bake in a preheated, 400-degree oven, uncovered, on the middle rack, 15 to 20 minutes. Remove from oven and let rest 10 minutes, then serve with additional gravy.

    NOTE: Manicotti may be prepared in advance, refrigerated, and baked prior to serving. Stuffed peppers and a salad complement this elegant meal nicely.

Serves 8–10

Baked Stuffed Ziti

This dish can be varied according to the sauce you use in it. If you use my Marinara Sauce, you will have a very light dish, which will be almost pink in color. If you want a more filling dish, one that is practically a complete meal, use the Tomato Gravy with Ground Meat or the Sunday Gravy. It will then have a dark color. (For recipes, see sauce chapter.)

> *1 pound ziti or any large macaroni*
> *1 recipe for sauce or gravy (see introduction above)*
> *1 pound ricotta cheese*
> *8 ounces grated mozzarella cheese, plus more for topping*
> *¼ cup freshly grated Parmesan cheese, plus more for topping*

2 large eggs
salt and pepper to taste
2 tablespoons chopped fresh parsley

1. Cook pasta according to directions, stirring often. Drain well and turn into a large bowl. Toss with a ladleful of sauce to keep it from sticking together.
2. Combine the ricotta, mozzarella, Parmesan, eggs, salt, and pepper. Using a whisk, mix until well blended. Add to the cooked, hot pasta. Toss lightly with a wooden spoon. Turn into a medium-size baking pan with a little sauce added to the bottom to prevent the pasta from scorching.
3. Spread a layer of sauce over the pasta. Top with mozzarella and Parmesan. Sprinkle with the chopped parsley. Cover with foil.
4. Bake in a preheated 350-degree oven on the middle rack for 25 minutes. Allow it to rest for 10 minutes before serving. Serve with the remaining hot sauce.

   NOTE: This dish should normally be prepared just prior to eating it. But it can be kept in the refrigerator after cooking for up to three days. To reheat, put 1 heaping tablespoon of water and $1/4$ cup of sauce in the bottom of a heavy skillet. Put baked ziti into the skillet, cover, and steam on low heat until thoroughly heated.

Serves 6–8

Insalata di Ziti
IIIIIII
Cold Ziti Salad

This is a delicious lunch dish or dinner appetizer.

3/4 pound smooth ziti (no lines)
1 small can tuna fish (about 1/4 pound) mashed
12 pitted black olives
8 stuffed green olives
1 sweet red pepper, diced
4 tablespoons olive oil

1 tablespoon white vinegar
2 hard-boiled eggs, quartered
1 large firm tomato, sliced

1. Cook the pasta in plenty of boiling salted water. Drain and reserve.
2. Meanwhile, prepare and mix together the tuna, black and green olives, and red pepper.
3. Add the pasta to the mixture and toss with the oil and vinegar.
4. Place onto a large platter and garnish with the quartered eggs and sliced tomato.

Serves 4

Lasagne Imbottite

IIIIIII

Baked Lasagne

Lasagne is a wonderful company dish, for the simple fact that it can be prepared in advance and baked just prior to serving. The tomato sauce recipe given here is a quick sauce to prepare. If you are also serving a roast for your dinner, this is the sauce you will want to use. If you want a more filling dish, use the Sunday Gravy or Tomato Gravy with Ground Meat (see sauce chapter).

Lasagne Tomato Sauce

¼ cup olive oil
1 small onion, chopped
1 garlic clove, chopped
1 6-ounce can tomato paste
1 14-ounce can peeled and crushed tomatoes
1 14-ounce can hot water
pinch of dried red pepper flakes, basil, mint, and oregano
salt and pepper to taste

1. Heat the olive oil. Add the onion and garlic and saute for about 3 minutes. Do not allow them to burn.
2. Add the tomato paste and stir until dissolved. Add the tomatoes and mix well. Add the hot water, stir well, and let the mixture come to a soft boil.
3. Add the seasonings, stir until they are blended, and let the sauce simmer while you prepare the lasagne. Or, if you wish, the sauce may be made as much as a day or two in advance and refrigerated before you finish the lasagne.

To Finish Preparation

2 tablespoons salt
1 tablespoon olive oil
1 pound lasagne noodles
2 pounds ricotta cheese
3 eggs
1 garlic clove, pressed (optional)
1¾ cups freshly grated Parmesan or Romano cheese
¼ cup chopped fresh parsley
salt and pepper to taste
¾ pound mozzarella cheese, shredded

1. Combine the salt and olive oil with 8 quarts of rapidly boiling water. Add the noodles and cook about 15 minutes or until tender. Stir constantly with a wooden spoon to prevent sticking. Do not overcook. Drain and rinse under cold water and reserve.
2. Meanwhile, combine the ricotta cheese, eggs, garlic, ¾ cup grated cheese, parsley, salt, and pepper in a large bowl. Mix well.
3. Bring the tomato sauce, ricotta filling, and cooked noodles to a clean working surface. Set out a 9 x 13-inch baking dish.
4. Pour ½ cup of the tomato sauce into the bottom of the baking pan. Over this, place a layer of lasagne noodles (you may slightly overlap). Top with 1 cup tomato sauce. Spread one-third of the ricotta mixture here and there, reaching the edges of the pan. Sprinkle ⅓ of the

Parmesan and mozzarella on the top. Start again with the noodles and repeat the layering process two more times until all the ingredients have been used. Now top with more tomato sauce and grated Parmesan cheese.

5. Bake in a preheated 350-degree oven for 40 minutes. Let rest for about 15 minutes so the noodles will settle and cut easily. Cut into 2-inch squares and serve with the remaining sauce, heated, and more grated cheese.

NOTE: Lasagne can be prepared early in the day on which it will be served and baked prior to serving.

Serves 6–8

Spaghetti with Lemon and Asparagus Sauce

IIIIIIII

salt
8 ounces spaghetti
6 tablespoons butter
8 fresh asparagus spears, peeled and cut into
   1-inch lengths
zest of 1 lemon
2 large eggs
3/4 cup heavy cream
2 tablespoons freshly grated Parmesan cheese
4 grates of nutmeg
3 tablespoons chopped fresh parsley
juice of 1 lemon
freshly ground pepper

1. Bring 3½ quarts of water to a rolling boil in a large pot. Stir in 1 tablespoon of salt. Add the spaghetti, stir, and cook it *al dente*, for about 6 minutes. Stir often.
2. Melt the butter in a medium-size frying pan. Add the asparagus pieces and cook them over medium heat for about 6 minutes. Meanwhile, finely grate the zest of 1 lemon.
3. Add the eggs, heavy cream, Parmesan cheese, nutmeg, parsley and half of the lemon juice; combine well. Taste the

sauce. The lemon flavor should be subtle but not over-powering. Add more lemon juice as needed.

4. Drain the spaghetti well. Immediately return it to the pot it was cooked in and add the butter, asparagus, and the lemon sauce. Toss well.

5. Turn the heat to low and continue gently tossing the pasta over the heat for about 30 seconds, until the sauce thickens slightly and adheres to the pasta. Season to taste with salt and pepper and serve immediately.

Serves 3 as a main course
Serves 6 as an appetizer

Frittata di Spaghetti
IIIIIII
Spaghetti Pie

This is great for using up any leftover pasta, even if it has already been cooked. Excellent as a late-night snack!

> *¾ pound spaghetti (cooked)*
> *3 tablespoons melted butter*
> *1 cup grated Parmesan cheese*
> *2 eggs (beaten)*
> *salt and pepper*
> *chopped fresh parsley*
> *2–3 tablespoons olive oil*

You will need a good, heavy 12-inch skillet, preferably cast iron.

1. Cook the spaghetti according to the package directions, if not already cooked. Drain the spaghetti well and toss it with the butter, beaten eggs, Parmesan cheese, salt and pepper to taste, and chopped parsley. Mix thoroughly.

2. Put the olive oil in a heavy skillet. When the oil is hot, pour in the spaghetti mixture and shape it into a round pie.

3. Using medium heat, gently work the pasta so that it browns evenly, by gently turning it around in the same direction to avoid sticking.

4. When one side is brown, slide the omelette onto a large plate; return it to the skillet to allow other side to brown. Add another tablespoon of oil if needed.
5. Leave the omelette to cool slightly before serving for a better flavor. Cut into wedges and serve with crusty Italian bread.

Serves 4

Fettuccine

IIIIIIII

Fettuccine is good with Tomato Gravy with Ground Meat or Pesto Sauce (see the sauce chapter) or a mixture of butter, grated cheese, and chopped fresh parsley. The pasta can be made ahead and covered with lots of flour and a clean cloth before it is cooked. Uncooked fettuccine also freezes well when placed in a freezer in single layers on a cookie sheet and then placed in a plastic bag.

> *6 cups unbleached flour (King Arthur preferred)*
> *1 teaspoon salt*
> *3 eggs*
> *about ¹/₂ cup boiling water*

1. Pour 5 cups of flour on a smooth working surface. Make a well in the center. Sprinkle with the teaspoon of salt. Drop the eggs in the well, break the yolks with your fingers, and stir a bit. Then mix the flour and eggs together until they form a cornmeal texture. Gradually mix in boiling water, using as much as necessary to form a smooth, pliable dough. Be careful you don't burn your hands. Always throw the flour on the water before touching it with your hands. This will cool it off a bit.
2. Knead the dough for about 10 minutes, until it is shiny and smooth. Form it into a loaf shape, pat the top with some water, and cover with an inverted bowl for a half hour.

3. Divide the dough in half, keeping the remainder covered. Roll the dough into a large round, about $1/8$ inch thick. Liberally sprinkle flour from the remaining cup of flour all over the dough to prepare for next step.
4. Starting at the top, gently fold over about 2 inches of dough. Continue to fold over dough so that the final width will be about 3 inches. The dough must be floured enough so that the layers do not stick together.
5. Beginning at one end of the roll, cut the dough into strips $1/4$ inch wide or a width you desire. (Be sure to use a sharp knife or the edges will be jagged.) Then sprinkle more flour on the cut pieces and gently toss them with your fingers until the noodles loosen and open to form long strands.
6. When you are ready to cook, boil the fettuccine in 6 quarts of water seasoned with 1 tablespoon salt. Boil gently, uncovered, stirring often, for about 5 to 7 minutes, or until tender.
7. Drain into a colander and then put in a large serving bowl. Cover with your chosen sauce and serve immediately.

Serves 8–10

Orange or Rosy Pasta

IIIIIIII

This colorful pasta is good with Marinara Sauce or Pesto Sauce (see the sauce chapter) or made "Alfredo" style. It also can be used for lasagne or manicotti. Experiment and make your own creation.

2 cups all-purpose flour (King Arthur unbleached preferred)
2 large eggs
3 tablespoons strained carrots or beets for babies, or tomato paste
boiling water

1. Mound 2 cups of flour on a work surface or in a large bowl and make a deep well in the center. Break the eggs into the well.
2. Beat the eggs lightly with a fork, and then stir in the carrots, beets, or tomato paste. Using a circular motion, mix the flour from the sides of the well into the eggs. If the dough is too crumbly to stick together, slowly add a few drops of boiling water.
3. Pat the dough into a ball and knead on a lightly floured surface for 10 minutes or until the dough is shiny-smooth and elastic. Cover and let rest for 20 minutes.
4. On a lightly floured surface, roll out one-fourth of the dough at a time to about $1/8$-inch thickness. Keep the unrolled portions covered with a large inverted bowl.
5. Cut and cook as described for Fettuccine.

Yield: 4 cups fettuccine

Spinach Pasta

IIIIIII

Spinach noodles are good with melted butter, plenty of grated cheese, and black pepper. Or be creative and use them with your favorite pasta sauce.

$1/2$ package (10-ounce size) frozen leaf spinach
$1/4$ cup water
pinch of salt
2 cups unbleached flour (King Arthur preferred)
2 large eggs

1. Cook the spinach in the salted water in a covered sauce-pan on medium heat for 5 minutes.
2. Meanwhile, mound the flour on a working surface or in a large bowl. Make a deep well in the center and break the eggs into the well.
3. Beat the eggs lightly with a fork. Using a circular motion, draw the flour from the sides of the well into the eggs. Gradually mix all the flour with the eggs.

4. Add the hot, undrained spinach (the juices will provide the water needed to make the dough). Being careful not to burn your hands, mix the spinach into the flour-egg mixture. If the dough is too crumbly to stick together, slowly add a few drops of hot, boiling water.
5. Pat the dough into a smooth ball and knead on a lightly floured surface for 10 minutes or until the dough is shiny-smooth and elastic. Cover and let rest for 20 minutes.
6. On a lightly floured surface, roll out one-fourth of the dough at a time to about ⅛-inch thickness. Keep the unrolled portions covered with a large inverted bowl.
7. Cut and cook as described for Fettuccine.

Yield: 4 cups fettuccine

Sal's Linguini alla Vongole en Bianco

Linguine with White Clam Sauce

This clam sauce can be made ahead and reheated. It refrigerates and freezes well. If you desire a more bountiful dish, add about ½ cup chopped mushrooms, canned or fresh, to the clams and continue cooking as directed. They work very well together.

6 tablespoons butter
1 garlic clove, chopped
1 shallot clove, chopped
3 scallions, sliced
4 shakes of Tabasco
½ large ripe tomato, quartered
squeeze of lemon
½ pound canned whole clams, or 12 fresh shucked clams (reserve juices)
2 pinches of chopped fresh parsley, plus more for garnish

¹/₃ cup dry white wine
¹/₂ pound thin linguine
freshly grated Romano cheese for garnish

1. Start heating a pot of salted water for the pasta, following package directions.
2. Heat 4 tablespoons of the butter in a small saucepan. Add the garlic, shallot, and scallions. Saute until transparent. Add the Tabasco, quartered tomato, and squeeze of lemon. Cook slowly for about 5 minutes. Add the reserved clam broth.
3. Raise the heat and let the mixture come to a boil. Then add the clams, chopped parsley, and white wine. Boil gently for a few minutes so that the clams are barely poached.
4. Put the pasta in the salted boiling water and cook for 7 minutes, or until *al dente*. Strain well by shaking the colander. Transfer to a deep serving dish, toss with the remaining 2 tablespoons of butter, and then pour the clam sauce on top. (Tossing the pasta with butter will prevent it from absorbing too much sauce.)
5. Sprinkle with chopped parsley and grated cheese and serve immediately.

Serves 2

Pasta with Broccoli Sauce

IIIIIIII

This pasta dish can be eaten hot or cold, as a side dish or a main course. The total preparation time is approximately 45 minutes.

1 bunch of broccoli (about 1¹/₂ pounds)
¹/₂ cup olive oil
4 garlic cloves, chopped
salt and pepper to taste

¹/₄ teaspoon dried red pepper flakes
3 cups warm water
¹/₂ pound pasta (ziti, gnocchi, or small shells)
*¹/₃ cup freshly grated Romano or Parmesan
cheese, plus more for garnish*

1. Cut off and discard about ¹/₂ inch of the end of the broccoli stem. Cut the broccoli into flowerets. Trim the tough leaves, peel the stems, and cut them into 1¹/₂-inch lengths. Set all the pieces aside.
2. Heat the oil in a heavy skillet or medium-size saucepan. Add the garlic, salt, pepper, and red pepper. Saute slowly on low heat until the garlic is lightly browned.
3. Remove the pan from the burner and gently pour in the 3 cups of warm water to start the sauce. Let the water-and-oil sauce boil briskly for a minute, then add the cut broccoli. Cook on medium heat to a soft boiling stage. Add more salt, pepper, and red pepper to taste.
4. Cook the pasta according to package directions, reserving some of the water before draining. (This can be added to sauce if more broth is desired.)
5. Put the drained pasta in a large skillet and pour the cooked broccoli sauce on top. Sprinkle with the grated cheese, cover, and simmer for 5 minutes or until the cheese is melted. Or to make it peasant-style (Ma's way), add the cooked pasta to the pan of broccoli, toss a couple of times until well mixed, then serve. Sprinkle each serving with more Parmesan or Romano cheese.

Serves 6

Fettuccine Alfredo Deluxe

||||||||

Fettuccine with Cream and Prosciutto

This is quite a delicacy when served as an appetizer for company or as a very nourishing main course. I like to use half egg noodles and half spinach noodles in it. *Pancetta* (a different kind of Italian ham) may be substituted for the prosciutto.

>*1/2 pound medium (1/8-inch-wide) fresh noodles*
>*1/2 cup heavy cream*
>*1 egg yolk*
>*1/2 cup melted butter or margarine, cooled*
>*1 cup freshly grated Parmesan or Romano cheese*
>*1/4 pound chopped prosciutto, trimmed of all fat*
>*8 black, dry-cured, Sicilian olives, pitted and sliced*
>*2 tablespoons chopped fresh parsley*

1. Have all the ingredients ready.
2. Cook the noodles in 3 quarts of rapidly boiling, salted water for about 3 minutes. Drain well, but do not rinse.
3. Meanwhile, in a large bowl, whisk together the heavy cream and the egg yolk. Slowly stir in the cooled melted butter or margarine.
4. Combine the noodles in the bowl with the cream mixture. Add the grated cheese, prosciutto, and black olives. Toss gently until all the noodles are coated. Sprinkle with the chopped parsley and serve immediately.

Serves 2–4

Fettuccine and Fresh Tomatoes Insalata

IIIIIII

This is a good way to use up some of your garden herbs and vegetables, or those of a generous neighbor. It can be served as a side dish or main course.

NOTE: Fresh tomatoes in season are the best material for Italian sauces. There is a lightness and a savor about them that can never be matched when canned tomatoes are used. Hothouse tomatoes, on the other hand, are too flavorless for this use.

> 6 large, ripe tomatoes
> salt and freshly ground black pepper to taste
> 2 garlic cloves, chopped
> 3/4 teaspoon Dijon-style mustard
> 1/2 cup olive oil
> 2 spring onions, trimmed and sliced thin
> 1/2 cup loosely packed chopped fresh parsley
> 1/2 cup loosely packed chopped fresh basil leaves
> 1/2 cup loosely packed chopped fresh mint leaves
> 1 pound fresh fettuccine noodles (half egg and
>   half spinach)
> 2 tablespoons butter
> 1 cup freshly grated Parmesan or Romano cheese
> about 8 pitted black olives, sliced in half
> 1 large 7–8 ounce can or jar roasted peppers,
>   sliced, for garnish (optional)

1. Core the tomatoes and put them in a roasting pan. Pour boiling hot water over them, and let them set for 1 minute. Then gently drain the tomatoes and rinse them with cold water. Let them rest for 1 minute.
2. Drain and peel the tomatoes. Cut them into slices, and cut each slice into strips. Pile the strips in a large bowl and add the olive oil. Add salt and pepper to taste. Set aside for 10 minutes.

3. Remove ¹/₄ cup of juice drippings from the tomatoes. Pour the juice into a separate bowl. Add the garlic and mustard to the juice and whisk to blend the mixture. Pour the dressing over the tomato strips and add the onions, parsley, basil, mint, and more salt and pepper to taste. Stir the tomato mixture gently and set aside for no longer than one hour.
4. Bring 6 quarts of salted water to a boil. Add the fresh fettuccine. Stir once or twice as the water returns to a boil. Then cook just until the pasta floats to the surface of the water (about 2 minutes) or until it is tender or *al dente*. Drain immediately, shake the colander to remove any excess water (do not rinse), and pile the pasta into a bowl.
5. Toss the pasta gently with the butter and then serve it onto dinner plates, forming a large nest of pasta on each plate.
6. Spoon some of the tomato sauce onto each plate and top with grated Parmesan, black olives, and pepper strips for garnish. Put the remaining tomato sauce in a serving pitcher for extra use.

Serves 4–6

Pasta con Acciughe

▌▌▌▌▌▌▌

Pasta with Anchovy Sauce

This sauce is especially good with green noodles.

¹/₂ pound egg or green noodles
2 tablespoons olive oil
2 tablespoons butter or margarine
2 garlic cloves, crushed
¹/₄ teaspoon dried basil

¹/₄ teaspoon dried red pepper flakes
6 black, Sicilian, dry-cured olives, pitted and
    halved
1 2-ounce can anchovy fillets, drained
2 tablespoons freshly grated Parmesan cheese
freshly ground black pepper to taste
chopped fresh parsley for garnish

1. Cook the noodles in boiling salted water until *al dente*.
2. Meanwhile, in a small saucepan over medium heat, warm the olive oil and butter with the garlic until the butter is melted and the garlic is golden brown. Add the basil, red pepper, olives, and anchovies. Stir with a wooden spoon to make a sauce.
3. Drain the pasta well and return it to the saucepan. Toss with the anchovy sauce and Parmesan cheese. (Be sure to use grated cheese sparingly as the anchovies can be a bit salty.) Place on a heated serving platter and top with black pepper to taste and some chopped parsley.

Serves 2–4

Rigatoni al Freddo
||||||||

Cold Rigatoni Salad

This is a good summer dish, especially good to have on hand when you need a quick bite to eat. It stores well in the refrigerator for several days.

¹/₂ cup olive oil
¹/₄ cup red or white wine vinegar
4 garlic cloves, finely chopped
1 tablespoon chopped fresh parsley
1 cup chopped fresh basil leaves
¹/₂ teaspoon salt
freshly ground black pepper to taste

10 red ripe tomatoes, or 2 cups canned peeled
   plum tomatoes (juice reserved)
1 pound rigatoni or ziti pasta with lines
¼ cup black, Sicilian, dry-cured olives, pitted
   (optional)
1 cup freshly grated Parmesan cheese for garnish

1. Combine the olive oil and vinegar in a large bowl and whisk until well blended. Add the garlic, parsley, basil, salt, and pepper, and stir well.
2. Peel the fresh tomatoes and slice them in small pieces. If you are using canned tomatoes, squeeze them slightly to remove as many seeds as possible, and then dice. Add the tomatoes to the oil and vinegar mixture, stir, and cover with plastic wrap. Marinate for a couple of hours. (Add the reserved tomato juice if this sauce looks too dry.)
3. Bring 6 quarts of salted water to a boil and add the pasta. Stirring often, bring it back to a soft boil, cooking about 7 minutes or until tender. Strain, rinse under cold water, and drain well, tossing the colander lightly. Transfer the pasta to a large serving platter.
4. Add the olives to the pasta. Spoon the tomato mixture on top and gently lift the pasta without disturbing the tomatoes, to allow some of the juices to pour into the pasta. Refrigerate until ready to use. Serve with grated Parmesan cheese.

Serves 4

Linguini ai Tre Formaggi
IIIIIIII

Linguine with Three Cheeses

Here is a good appetizer or side dish to serve with the meat of your choice. It will take a half hour to prepare and cook.

2 tablespoons olive oil
1 garlic clove
¼ cup chopped fresh Italian parsley
salt and freshly ground black pepper
1 pound linguine
½ cup crushed Gorgonzola cheese
¼ cup freshly grated Parmesan cheese
¼ cup freshly grated Romano or Pecorino *cheese*

1. Fill a large pot with 6 quarts of salted water and start heating it for the pasta.
2. Heat the oil in a large skillet, and push the garlic through a garlic press into the oil. Add part of the parsley and saute for a few minutes. Set the skillet aside until the pasta is cooked.
3. Add linguine to the rapidly boiling water. Cook the pasta until it is *al dente*. Drain the pasta, transfer it to the skillet, and toss with the garlic and oil mixture.
4. Put the skillet back on the burner. Add the three kinds of cheeses, a little at a time, and keep tossing until the entire amount is mixed into the pasta. Cook on medium heat for 3 minutes. Add more salt and pepper to taste, if needed, and the remaining parsley.
5. Serve immediately.

Serves 4–6

Mom's Pasta and Ricotta alla Romana

||||||||

The sauce for this pasta dish may be made ahead, but the pasta should be cooked immediately before serving.

½ pound fine linguine or spaghettini
½ pound fresh plum tomatoes, or 1 cup canned
*   plum tomatoes*
2 tablespoons olive oil

1 garlic clove
3 tablespoons minced fresh basil
¹/₄ cup chopped fresh Italian parsley
salt and freshly ground black pepper to taste
1 cup ricotta cheese
3 tablespoons freshly grated Parmesan cheese

1. Fill a large pot with 3 quarts of salted water and start heating it for the pasta.
2. Remove the hard portion of the fresh tomatoes near the stem. Chop the tomatoes until you have 1 cup. Reserve the juice in another cup. If you are using canned tomatoes, squeeze them to eliminate the seeds and reserve the juice.
3. When the water is rapidly boiling, add the pasta. Cook until tender or *al dente*, about 6 to 10 minutes.
4. While the pasta is cooking, heat the olive oil in a saucepan. Push the garlic through a garlic press into the oil, or mince it and add it to the oil. Saute for 1 minute on medium-low heat. Now add the chopped tomatoes, basil, parsley, salt, and pepper. Cook until the mixture is reduced to a sauce consistency. Add the reserved tomato juices if the sauce looks more dry than you like.
5. Drain the cooked pasta thoroughly (reserve some cooking water). Return the pasta to the pot. Pour in the tomato sauce and toss. Add the ricotta and toss again. Sprinkle with Parmesan cheese and serve at once. This produces a thick, cheesy dish. (If you prefer a moister consistency, use some of the reserved boiling water from the pasta and add as desired.)

Serves 2

Low-Calorie Pastiere

||||||||

Macaroni Pie

Macaroni Pie makes a light but filling lunch or dinner.

> *4 eggs*
> *1 pound small curd cottage cheese*
> *1 cup freshly grated Romano cheese*
> *½ cup chopped fresh parsley*
> *salt and pepper to taste*
> *4 cups cooked elbow macaroni*

1. In a large bowl, beat the eggs well. Add the cottage cheese, grated cheese, parsley, salt, and pepper. Mix well.
2. Now gently toss the elbow macaroni into the mixture.
3. Generously grease an 8 x12-inch glass or enamel baking dish. Add the macaroni mixture.
4. Bake in a preheated 325-degree oven for 1 hour or until a knife inserted in the center comes out clean.

Serves 4–6

Quick Primavera

||||||||

This *primavera* can be kept in the refrigerator for several days to be used for lunch, an appetizer, or a main course. It can be served cold or at room temperature.

> *1 pound ziti, rotini, or tortellini*
> *1 pound zucchini*
> *1 pound ripe plum tomatoes*
> *4 large mushrooms*
> *3 tablespoons vegetable oil*
> *6 shallots*

6 parsley sprigs, chopped
2 tablespoons minced fresh basil, or 1 tablespoon
  dried basil
1 small garlic clove, crushed
½ cup chopped cooked broccoli
pinch of dried oregano, mint, and red pepper
  flakes
salt and freshly ground black pepper to taste
¼ cup grated fresh Parmesan, Pecorino, *or*
  Romano cheese.

1. Fill a large pot with 6 quarts of water and start heating it for the pasta.
2. Wash and trim the zucchini, tomatoes, and mushrooms, but do not peel.
3. Pour the oil into a large skillet, but do not put the pan over the heat yet.
4. Dice the unpeeled zucchini and tomatoes into the oil and then dice the shallots. Slice the mushrooms into the mixture. Add the chopped parsley, basil, garlic, cooked broccoli, and pinch of oregano, mint, and red pepper flakes. Turn the heat to medium-high and cook, stirring often with a wooden spoon. After 5 minutes, add salt and pepper. Turn off the heat and reserve. By now, the water should be boiling for the pasta.
5. Cook the pasta according to package directions, or for less time for a firmer pasta. Gently strain the pasta when it is cooked and shake it briskly to remove excess water.
6. Transfer the pasta to a large serving platter. Pour the sauce over it, a small amount at a time, and toss with two forks to mix before adding more. Add half the grated cheese and toss again. Taste, and add more salt and pepper if needed.
7. Serve immediately, with the remaining cheese in a separate bowl to be used according to individual taste. Or refrigerate, covered, up to several days if desired.

Serves 8

Pasta Primavera Deluxe

IIIIIIII

What a wonderful way to use some leftover vegetables—
raw or cooked. Remember, the best part of this recipe is the
fact that you can replace any of the ingredients below with
your own leftovers. You also can eliminate some of the
vegetables if necessary. Pasta and vegetables are very com-
patible. Go ahead and experiment. You can't go wrong!
This recipe can be made ahead and refrigerated for several
days.

2 pounds tortellini or rotini pasta (3 colors)
mayonnaise
2 cups broccoli flowerets
1 cup cauliflowerets
¼ pound fresh green beans, ends trimmed and
*   snapped in half*
¼ pound small whole mushrooms
olive oil
wine vinegar
pinch of dried oregano
12 ounces canned, roasted red peppers, sliced
1 4-ounce jar of black, Sicilian, dry-cured olives,
*   pitted*
3 ounces canned flat anchovies, drained
chopped fresh parsley
2 large garlic cloves
pinch of dried red pepper flakes
salt and pepper to taste
3 tablespoons butter or margarine
1 bunch of asparagus, snapped into pieces
2 small zucchini, unpeeled, sliced
2 ripe tomatoes, chopped
2 shallot cloves, chopped
1 fresh basil leaf, chopped, or a pinch of dried
*   basil*
pinch of dried mint flakes
4 ounces canned chickpeas, drained
freshly grated Romano cheese

1. Cook the pasta *al dente*. Drain and toss with enough mayonnaise to coat. Reserve on a large serving platter.
2. Parboil the broccoli, cauliflower, and green beans, uncovered. Rinse under cold water and add to the pasta. If the vegetables are already cooked, briefly reheat them in a saute pan and cut them into bite-size pieces before adding them to the pasta. Raw vegetables can be used according to personal preference.
3. Boil the mushrooms for 3 minutes. Drain and toss with enough oil and wine vinegar to coat. Mix in a pinch of oregano and add to the pasta.
4. Place on a cutting surface the roasted peppers, olives, anchovies, 1 tablespoon of chopped parsley, and 1 garlic clove. Chop all together so the ingredients are evenly cut and distributed. Add to the pasta and toss lightly. Drizzle the mixture with olive oil and add black and red pepper to taste.
5. Melt the butter and saute the asparagus lightly. Remove with a slotted spoon and add to the pasta.
6. Saute the zucchini in the same skillet. Drain and add to the pasta.
7. Add more butter, if needed, to the skillet. Saute the tomatoes, the remaining garlic clove, chopped, the shallots, basil, mint, and more red pepper flakes, salt, and pepper to taste. This process should take no more than 3 minutes. Transfer the mixture to the pasta and toss gently again.
8. Add the chickpeas and additional mayonnaise as needed to moisten the entire mixture. Add a dash of wine vinegar to taste and more salt and pepper, if desired.
9. Refrigerate, covered, until ready to serve. Sprinkle with grated cheese and more chopped fresh parsley before serving. Serve chilled or at room temperature.

Serves 8

Potato Gnocchi

IIIIIII

Gnocchi, also known as dumplings, are a great delicacy. They can be served with any tomato sauce (see the sauce chapter) or substituted for the pasta in the Pasta with Broccoli Sauce recipe (see page 57). Top with plenty of freshly grated Parmesan cheese, black pepper, and dried red pepper flakes, and watch your family's delight! A salad and light wine will complete the meal. They also can be served as a side dish or appetizer.

> *1 pound potatoes*
> *2 cups King Arthur unbleached flour*

1. Wash, pare, and cube the potatoes. Cover them completely with boiling salted water, cover the pot, and cook about 20 minutes or until tender when pierced with a fork. Drain the potatoes, but do not rinse them with cold water; they should remain boiling hot. Reserve some hot water for further use.
2. Put the cooked potatoes on a flat working surface and mash. Immediately measure the flour on top of the potatoes and mix well to make a soft elastic dough.
3. Knead the dough well until it is pliable, adding some of the reserved hot water if needed. To knead the dough, fold the opposite side over toward you. Using the heel of your hand, gently push the dough away from you. Give it a quarter turn, always turning in the same direction. Repeat the process rhythmically until the dough is smooth and elastic (5 to 8 minutes), using as little additional flour as possible.
4. To make gnocchi, break off small pieces of dough. Using the palm of your hand, roll the pieces to pencil thickness. Cut them into pieces about ¾ inch long. Curl each piece by pressing lightly with your index finger and pulling your finger along the piece of dough toward you. Gnocchi may also be shaped by pressing each piece lightly with a floured fork to form an indentation.

5. Bring 3 quarts of salted water to a boil. Add gnocchi gradually, a few pieces at a time. Boil rapidly, uncovered, for about 8 to 10 minutes, or until tender. Drain. Top with sauce of your choice and serve.

NOTE: Gnocchi freeze well. Place the bits of dough on a cookie sheet, freeze, then drop into a plastic bag. When you're ready to cook, just drop them into the boiling water as usual.

Serves 6–8

Tarrali

IIIIIII

Italian Bagels

A family favorite and hard to come by. Please enjoy.

> *6 eggs*
> *½ cup oil*
> *1 package dry yeast*
> *4 cups flour, divided (1 cup and 3 cups)*
> *1 heaping teaspoon pepper*

1. In a large mixing bowl, beat the eggs thoroughly; add the oil and beat again.
2. Mix the yeast with 1 cup of the flour; then beat into the first mixture. Add the remaining flour gradually, along with the pepper, mixing well. Knead the dough thoroughly.
3. Break off 24 small pieces and roll out or pull into pencil shape. Press the ends together to make a circle.
4. Place in boiling water a few at a time and cook until they come to the surface of the water. Remove from the water and let cool.
5. When cool, bake on ungreased cookie sheets at 350 degrees for 25 minutes, until golden brown and dry.

   NOTE: If you wish, you may add more pepper than the recipe calls for.

Yield: 24 *tarrali*

Pizza, Calzone, and Polenta

||||||||||

Pizza

▌▌▌▌▌▌▌

Pizza is certainly the most perfect food. When I was a young girl, my mother would give me my allowance of 35 cents every Friday, and I would visit the pizza parlor to order a pizza to go. A whole pizza (they really made them much smaller then) for myself! I always loved my mother, but never as much as when I bit into my Friday treat. To this day I feel like a little girl whenever I sit down to my own pizza pie.

Basic Pizza Dough

3/4 cup lukewarm water
1 package dry yeast
1/8 teaspoon sugar
3 cups unbleached flour (King Arthur brand gives
   a quality lift)
1 teaspoon salt
1/4 cup olive oil
vegetable oil

1. Place the lukewarm water in a small bowl and sprinkle the yeast and sugar over it. Let stand in a warm, draft-free place for 10 to 15 minutes, until a foam forms on top.
2. In a large bowl, combine 1 cup of the flour and the teaspoon of salt.
3. Add the olive oil to the yeast mixture. Pour the mixture into the bowl of flour.
4. Gradually add the second cup of flour, stirring with a wooden spoon. When the dough begins to pull away from the sides of the bowl, turn it out onto a floured board.
5. Gradually knead the rest of the flour into the dough until the dough is smooth, elastic, and no longer sticky (about 10 minutes). The amount of flour needed will vary, depending on how moist the dough is and on the weather; a damp or humid day will cause excess moisture.

6. Coat a medium-size bowl with vegetable oil and place the ball of dough in it, rolling to coat it on all sides. Cover it tightly with plastic wrap and set in a warm place until it has doubled in bulk, about 45 to 60 minutes. To test if the dough has doubled, gently press two fingers into it; if they leave impressions, the dough is ready. While the dough is rising, prepare the sauce.

Basic Pizza Sauce

¼ cup olive oil
1 garlic clove, crushed
1 tablespoon tomato paste
1 8-ounce can peeled and crushed tomatoes
pinch of dried oregano, red pepper flakes, basil, and mint
salt and freshly ground black pepper to taste

1. Heat the oil in a saucepan and add the garlic. Simmer on low heat until the garlic is golden brown, but not burned.
2. Add the tomato paste and stir to mix well. Add the tomatoes with their juice, herbs, salt, and pepper. Bring to a soft boil, stirring often, and let simmer 10 to 20 minutes.

NOTE: The sauce can be made ahead and then reheated when it is needed. The recipe makes about 1½ cups of sauce.

To Finish Pizza

olive oil
3 Italian sausages, fried until lightly browned and sliced (optional)
¼ pound pepperoni, sliced (optional)
1 medium-size green bell pepper, seeded and sliced in thin rings (optional)
¼ pound thinly sliced mushrooms (optional)
½ to 1 can anchovy fillets, drained (optional)
1 medium Bermuda onion, thinly sliced (optional)
½ pound shredded mozzarella cheese

¹/₂ cup freshly grated Parmesan or Romano cheese

1. Preheat the oven to 450 degrees. (To produce a heavenly, crispy pizza, the first thing to remember is that a very hot oven is very important! This will brown the crust and cook the sauce quickly so it will not seep through the dough.)
2. Lightly flour a clean flat surface, enough so that the dough does not stick. Flatten the dough with your hands until it forms a circle. Start punching it all around with the back of a clenched fist to shape it into a large 14- to 15-inch circle, sprinkling it with flour as needed. Make a rim all around the circle, using your fingertips.
3. Rub 1 tablespoon of olive oil onto the surface of a large pizza pan. Arrange the circle of dough on the pan.
4. Add the pizza sauce to the center of the dough and spread it almost to the edges. Scatter over the entire dough, as desired, the sausages, pepperoni, pepper, mushrooms, anchovies, and onion slices. Top with the mozzarella and Parmesan or Romano cheeses.
5. Drizzle olive oil evenly over the entire pizza. Put the pizza on the top rack of the 450-degree oven. Let it cook for 20 minutes. This will seal the crust and tomatoes immediately and heat the oil on the bottom of the pan to cook the dough. When the dough is golden, move the pizza to the middle rack, lower the oven temperature a little, and cook 10 to 15 minutes.

Serves 2–6

Calzone

||||||||

This is a delicious warm lunch, or it can be served cold on a summer's day. When I serve it warm, I sometimes top it with a dab of marinara sauce for a scrumptious taste. All that is needed to complete the meal is a tossed salad.

1 1-pound chunk of prosciutto or boiled ham,
  cubed
2 pounds ricotta cheese, drained if very wet
1 cup freshly grated Parmesan or Romano cheese
3 eggs
salt and pepper to taste
Basic Pizza Dough (page 74)
olive oil
¹/₂ pound mozzarella, cubed
1 cup homemade or canned tomato sauce

1. Using a large bowl, mix ham or prosciutto, ricotta, grated cheese, eggs, salt, and pepper (the cheese will produce a salty taste, so test carefully). Set this filling aside.
2. Stretch the dough to make a 12- to 14-inch round. Leave dough slightly thick so that the filling will not ooze out.
3. Put the dough on a lightly oiled pizza pan, avoiding the edges. Gently spoon the filling onto half the pizza round. Fold the other half of dough over to form a large turnover. Use your fingertips to press the edges tightly together until all the dough is sealed.
4. Moisten the top and sides of the calzone with olive oil, using a pastry brush or the palm of your hand to spread it evenly. Cut a few slits in the middle of the calzone. Place some cubes of mozzarella and a ladleful or two of tomato sauce in each of these slits. Use all the cheese and sauce.
5. Bake the calzone in a preheated 350-degree oven for 40 to 45 minutes or until golden brown. It is best to use the medium rack of the oven.
6. Let the calzone rest for at least 20 minutes to allow the cheese mixture to set. Cut in slices and serve as an appetizer or as a lunch dish, topped with additional tomato sauce if desired.

Serves 4–6

Calzone with Spinach-Ricotta Filling

IIIIIII

Calzone is great with a variety of ingredients. Many of my friends layer it with salami, baked ham, Provolone cheese—sort of an Italian sub. It is good with any vegetables, such as broccoli, mushrooms, or spinach. Once you become accustomed to preparing this wonderful food, you will become more creative with it.

> *1 cup firmly packed spinach leaves, washed and*
> *dried*
> *1 cup ricotta cheese*
> *¹/₂ cup freshly grated Parmesan cheese*
> *1 egg yolk*
> *1 garlic clove, pressed*
> *salt and freshly grated black pepper to taste*
> *Basic Pizza Dough (page 74)*
> *olive oil*
> *¹/₂ pound mozzarella, cubed*

1. Finely mince the spinach leaves and blend with the ricotta cheese, Parmesan cheese, egg yolk, garlic clove, and salt and pepper.
2. Prepare and fill the dough as directed on the previous calzone recipe. Brush the top and sides of the calzone with olive oil. Cut a few slits in the middle of the calzone. Place the cubes of mozzarella in each of these slits.
3. Bake the calzone in a preheated 350-degree oven on the middle rack for 40 to 45 minutes, or until golden brown.
4. Let the calzone rest for at least 20 minutes before serving to allow the cheese mixture to set.

Serves 4–6

Claire's Pepperoni Pie

∎∎∎∎∎∎∎

My high school friend Claire used to serve Pepperoni Pie as an appetizer when we had one of our gatherings at her house. It is also good as a one-step meal, similar to a quiche.

> *3/4 cup diced pepperoni*
> *3/4 cup cubed Muenster cheese*
> *3/4 cup flour*
> *2 eggs*
> *1 cup milk*

1. Place all the ingredients in a small bowl in the order given.
2. Stir with a slotted spoon until the batter is smooth. The mixture should be lumpy only because of the pepperoni and cheese.
3. Pour the batter into a greased 9-inch pie plate.
4. Bake in a preheated 400-degree oven for 30–35 minutes or until the center is firm (test with a toothpick).
5. Cut into wedges and serve.

Serves 6–8

Polenta

∎∎∎∎∎∎∎

Polenta can be cooked to the consistency of cream of wheat and eaten with milk and honey or butter and cheese. Leftovers can be cut into slices that are fried, broiled, baked, or toasted and served with a variety of sauces and fillings. Like pasta or rice, polenta accents and absorbs any flavor it is matched with. It can be used in appetizers, side dishes, or main courses. For example, try this hors d'oeuvre: On skewers, alternate cubes of leftover polenta and fontina cheese that have been dipped in beaten egg and rolled in seasoned bread crumbs; deep-fry and serve hot. Or, for a hearty inexpensive meal on a cold winter night, serve polenta the old-fashioned Italian way. Spread it on a large board in the middle of the table and top it with cacciatore sauce and freshly grated Parmesan cheese. Seat your family or guests around the table, pour the wine, and have each person pick a corner and start eating.

1³/₄ cups yellow cornmeal
2 cups cold water
1 teaspoon salt
5 cups water
3 tablespoons olive oil
melted butter or fontina cheese

1. In a bowl, combine the cornmeal, cold water, and salt. Mix and set aside.
2. In a large heavy pot, bring the 5 cups of water to a boil. Add the oil and stir in the cornmeal mixture. Always stir clockwise. With a wire whisk, beat the cornmeal until it thickens, about 5 minutes. This will keep the polenta smooth and free of lumps. Cook it over medium heat, stirring *constantly* with a wooden spoon for 30 minutes. Use a wooden spoon with the longest handle you can find and wear long sleeves, for polenta will bubble and can splatter. If the batter gets too thick, add a ladleful of water and continue stirring.
3. When the polenta is the consistency of cream of wheat, cover the pot and leave it on the heat for 3 minutes more without stirring. Shake the pot a little; this will allow some steam to get under the polenta so it will detach itself from the bottom of the pot easily. Then turn the polenta onto a smooth surface or into a lightly oiled round bowl. The polenta should be allowed to set and become firm enough to cut, but it should still be warm when it is served.
4. Cover the polenta with melted butter or fontina cheese. To cut it, use a wooden spatula if you have one, or a piece of string or dental floss. It is customary to avoid anything metal, however, because the taste of metal will destroy the taste of polenta.

5. Serve with additional salt and pepper to pass around, dried red pepper flakes, and grated Romano or *Pecorino* cheese.

Serves 6–8

Sausage Gravy for Polenta

IIIIIII

Since cornmeal is bland when it stands alone, sausage gravy does a great job of sprucing it up. This is only one of many ways polenta can be served.

> *1 pound Italian sausages, hot or sweet as desired*
> *2 tablespoons water*
> *2 tablespoons olive oil*
> *1 small onion, chopped*
> *1 garlic clove, chopped*
> *2¹/₂ cups canned peeled Italian plum tomatoes*
> *pinch of dried red pepper flakes, basil, and mint*
> *salt and pepper to taste*

1. Fry the sausages with the 2 tablespoons of water in a large heavy skillet over medium heat until dry. Then, prick the sausages with a fork and let them brown in their own juices. When they are brown, remove with a slotted spoon and set aside.
2. Drain the fat and add the olive oil to the pan. When the oil is warm, brown the chopped onion and garlic. Raise the heat to high and add the tomatoes, which have been squeezed in your hands to crush them. Stir until bubbly.
3. Add sausages and seasonings. Simmer for 20 minutes or until the sausages are cooked, stirring frequently with a wooden spoon.
4. Place the sausages around the platter of polenta with plenty of grated cheese. Pour the gravy on top of the polenta. Cut the polenta as described in the polenta recipe and serve.

Serves 3–4

Meat and Poultry Dishes

IIIIIIII

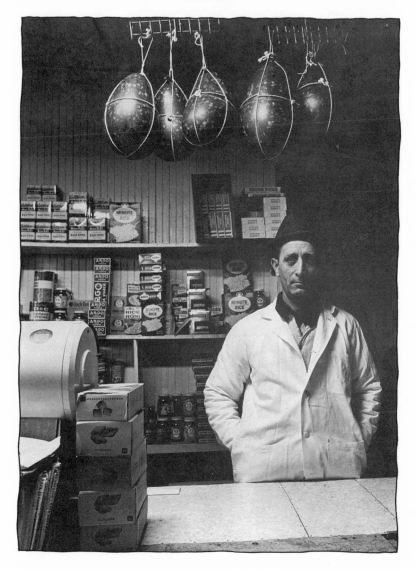

Veal Scaloppini

IIIIIII

This is a favorite in most Italian restaurants, including my brother's restaurant, Dom's, in the North End. The secret of this recipe is to have all the ingredients on hand and to work quickly.

> *6 tablespoons unsalted butter*
> *6 2-ounce veal scallops*
> *flour to coat veal*
> *salt and pepper to taste*
> *chopped fresh parsley for garnish*

1. Using a medium-high heat, melt the butter in a saute pan.
2. Lightly dredge the veal with flour, shaking off the excess.
3. When the butter is hot but not burning, place the veal in the saute pan. Lightly brown the slices on one side, turn them over, and cook quickly, 1 minute or so, on the other side. You must work fast to produce a tender veal.
4. Transfer the veal slices to a warm platter. Stir the sauce well, scraping up any bits that may be stuck to the pan. Pour it over the veal.
5. Season with salt and pepper and sprinkle with fresh parsley. Serve immediately with buttered pasta or rice.

Serves 2

Veal Marsala

IIIIIII

Have all the ingredients nearby and ready. Work quickly! Once you are prepared, this dish can be cooked and served in less than 10 minutes.

> *6 tablespoons unsalted butter*
> *6 2-ounce veal scallops*

flour to coat veal
salt and pepper to taste
2 shallots, chopped
3 or 4 ounces Marsala wine
6 fresh mushrooms, thinly sliced
chopped fresh parsley for garnish

1. Using a medium-high heat, melt the butter in a saute pan.
2. Lightly dredge the veal with flour, shaking off any excess.
3. Place the veal in the saute pan and lightly brown on one side. Sprinkle with salt and pepper, turn over, and add chopped shallots. Cook 1 minute more.
4. On high heat, add the Marsala and boil rapidly to burn off the excess alcohol. Add the mushrooms and cook briefly to blend flavors.
5. Transfer the veal to a warm platter. Pour the sauce over the veal, sprinkle with chopped parsley, and serve immediately.

Serves 2

IIII Use seasonal foods for the appropriate recipes, for they will be the least expensive and the most readily available. **IIII**

Veal and Peppers

IIIIIII

1½ pounds lean veal
olive oil
3 large cloves garlic, peeled
3 large bell peppers, chopped
2 large white onions, chopped
salt and pepper
red pepper flakes (optional)
fresh parsley, chopped

1. Have butcher slice the veal ¼ inch thick as for cutlets. Cut into ¼ inch slices.
2. Cover the bottom of a 12-inch frying pan with olive oil to a depth of ¼ inch. Slice garlic cloves lengthwise into thirds and saute slowly over low heat until translucent. Do not burn. Remove the garlic.
3. Add the veal; turn heat to medium-high and immediately add the peppers and onions; cover.
4. Cook for 1½ minutes; turn the veal, lower heat, and continue to cook until done (approximately another 3 minutes).
5. Season to taste with salt, pepper, and red pepper flakes if desired. Sprinkle with fresh parsley.

Serves 2–4

Veal and Mushrooms Cacciatore

IIIIIII

6 veal shoulder steaks
½ cup flour seasoned with oregano and parsley
3 tablespoons olive oil
2 cloves garlic, crushed
1 can whole tomatoes, drained
salt and pepper
2 tablespoons chopped parsley
1 15-ounce can mushrooms, drained (reserve juice), OR ¼ pound fresh mushrooms

1. Dredge the steaks in the seasoned flour. Shake off the excess flour.
2. Heat the oil in a heavy skillet; cook the crushed garlic in the oil gently until golden brown.
3. Add the steaks and cook until brown on both sides.
4. Add the mushrooms to the meat. Cover and cook for 5 minutes.
5. Add the tomatoes, juice from canned mushrooms, and parsley; simmer gently until the steaks are tender.

Serves 4–6

Veal Piccata

▌▌▌▌▌▌▌
Veal with Prosciutto

¹/₄ cup unsalted butter
1 pound veal scallops
2 tablespoons flour
salt and freshly ground black pepper
¹/₈ pound prosciutto, sliced very thin and slivered
2 tablespoons stock
1 tablespoon butter
1 teaspoon chopped fresh parsley
2 teaspoons lemon juice

1. Heat the butter in a frying pan.
2. Dredge the meat in flour, salt, and pepper.
3. Place the meat in the frying pan and cook over high heat for 2 minutes on each side. Transfer the meat to a warm platter and keep it in a warm place.
4. Place the prosciutto in the frying pan and cook it 3 minutes, stirring quickly. Remove it from the pan and place it over the veal.
5. Add the stock, butter, and parsley to the pan gravy. Scrape the pan well, cook for 2 minutes, and add the lemon juice.
6. Pour the sauce over the meat. Serve immediately with sauteed sliced zucchini or squash.

Serves 4

Veal Cutlet Parmigiana

||||||||

If you wish, you can fry the cutlets early in the day, then bake them in the sauce just prior to serving. Spaghetti makes a good accompaniment, and a tossed salad and Italian bread round out the meal. Boneless chicken breasts may be substituted.

1 egg, beaten
1 cup milk
1/2 pound bread crumbs
3 tablespoons freshly grated Parmesan cheese
1 tablespoon chopped fresh parsley
salt and pepper to taste
1 pound veal cutlets
1 cup olive oil
2 cups any meatless tomato sauce (see recipes in sauce chapter)
8 ounces shredded mozzarella cheese

1. Combine the egg and milk in one bowl. In another bowl, mix the bread crumbs, 1 tablespoon of the grated Parmesan, parsley, salt, and pepper. Dip each cutlet first into the egg wash and then into the bread crumb mixture. Press the slices gently so that the crumbs will adhere to the meat on both sides.
2. Heat the oil in a heavy frying pan. Add the cutlets when the oil is good and hot. Fry the cutlets slowly on both sides until they are golden brown.
3. Place the cutlets on a heavy baking sheet or pan. Pour the tomato sauce over each cutlet and sprinkle with the remaining grated Parmesan and the mozzarella. Bake 10 to 15 minutes in a preheated 375-degree oven, or until the mozzarella has melted.

Serves 4

Veal Piccante

▌▌▌▌▌▌▌

Veal with Anchovies

2 ounces unsalted butter
6 2-ounce veal scallops
flour to dredge veal
6 flat anchovies, drained and chopped
12 capers (in water), drained
½ lemon
freshly ground black pepper
chopped fresh parsley

1. Heat the butter in a saute pan over medium-high heat.
2. Dredge the veal in flour and shake off the excess.
3. Place the veal in the pan and lightly brown on one side. Turn it over, raise the heat to high, and add the anchovies and capers. Let the mixture get red hot.
4. Squeeze the half lemon (juice only) over the veal. Add pepper to taste. Shake pan vigorously, sprinkle the veal with parsley, and serve immediately.

Serves 2

▐▐ To make fresh bread crumbs, use day-old Italian bread. Cut any leftover pieces into small chunks, and put a few chunks in the blender at a time. Blend just until you have light and fluffy crumbs, which in turn will produce a delicate stuffing. ▐▐

Veal Stew with Tomatoes and Peas

IIIIIIII

The aroma of this meal will make your neighbors come knocking. Don't be surprised if they linger until dinnertime. A good loaf of Italian bread will complement this hearty winter meal.

> 1 1/2 pounds boned shoulder of veal
> 1/2 cup olive oil
> 2 garlic cloves, mashed
> 3/4 cup flour
> 1/2 teaspoon dried marjoram
> salt and pepper to taste
> 1 cup dry white wine
> 1 tablespoon chopped fresh parsley
> 1 bay leaf
> 1 14-ounce can tomatoes, or 2 large ripe
>   tomatoes, seeded and chopped
> 1 cup fresh peas, or 1 10-ounce package of frozen
>   small peas, thawed

1. Cut the veal into cubes for stewing.
2. Place the oil in a large stew pan, add the garlic, and brown gently. Discard the garlic.
3. Spread the flour on waxed paper. Dip the pieces of veal in the flour, coating them on all sides. Shake off the excess flour.
4. Add the veal to the pan with the marjoram, salt, and pepper. Over medium-high heat, brown the veal thoroughly on all sides. When the meat is well browned, add the wine, parsley, and bay leaf. Cook slowly until the wine evaporates.
5. Add the tomatoes, enough warm water to cover the meat, and more seasonings as needed. Stir gently, scraping up any residue on the bottom of the pan. When the tomato sauce begins to boil, cover the pot and set the heat to simmer. Cook slowly until the veal is very tender, about 1 hour.

6. When the veal has been cooking for about 45 minutes, add the peas and adjust seasonings for taste. More water may be added during cooking time if necessary. Remove the bay leaf before serving.

Serves 4

Ossobuco

IIIIIIII

Ossobuco means, literally, "bone with a hole," and refers to the fact that the veal shanks are sawed crosswise, exposing the marrow-filled hole through the middle of the bone. This is the way my brother Dom and his wife, Toni-Lee, serve *Ossobuco* in Dom's Restaurant.

> *¹/₂ cup butter*
> *¹/₂ cup chopped onions*
> *¹/₂ cup chopped celery*
> *¹/₂ cup chopped carrots*
> *1 garlic clove, minced*
> *1 heaping tablespoon chopped fresh parsley*
> *about ¹/₂ cup flour*
> *salt and pepper to taste*
> *3 veal shanks, cut in half*
> *¹/₂ cup olive oil*
> *¹/₂ cup white wine*
> *¹/₂ cup chicken broth*
> *1 bay leaf*
> *2 cups canned chopped Italian plum tomatoes, strain juices*

1. Melt the butter in a large Dutch oven over medium heat. When it is hot, but not burning, add the onions, celery, and carrots. Stir often. When the onions are transparent, turn off the heat. Add the garlic and parsley and stir for a few minutes.

2. Put about ¹/₂ cup of flour in a paper bag. Add salt and pepper and the veal shanks. Shake the bag vigorously. Shake the excess flour from the shanks.

3. In a separate skillet, brown the shanks in the olive oil. Remove them from the skillet and place them on top of the vegetables in the Dutch oven.

4. Use the drippings in the skillet as a base for your sauce. Start by pouring out any excess fat. Add the wine to the remaining drippings and cook rapidly, until the mixture thickens.

5. Now add the broth, bay leaf, and tomatoes. Bring the sauce to a boil. Then, pour it over the veal and vegetables in the Dutch oven.

6. Cover the Dutch oven and bake in a preheated 350-degree oven for 1¹/₂ hours. Baste often. Add more broth if it starts to dry out, but do not drown the veal shanks. The sauce should be fairly thick.

7. Remove the bay leaf before serving. Serve freshly cooked noodles.

   NOTE: *Ossobuco* may be prepared in advance, refrigerated for 2 or 3 days, and reheated before serving.

Serves 4

Ossobuco Milanese Style

IIIIIIII

This dish has been showing up on a lot of restaurant menus lately, although it frequently requires advance notice. The meat is succulent, and don't forget to eat the marrow in the bones. It is both nutritious and delicious!

> *1 tablespoon butter*
> *4 veal shin bones, 4 inches long, with meat*
> *2 tablespoons flour*
> *salt and pepper to taste*
> *¹/₂ cup dry white wine*
> *1 cup water*

1 teaspoon chopped fresh parsley
½ garlic clove, chopped
4 strips lemon peel, 1 inch long
1 anchovy fillet, chopped
1 tablespoon broth
1 tablespoon butter

1. Heat the tablespoon of butter in a deep heavy skillet.
2. Roll the bones in the flour. Place them in the skillet, add salt and pepper, and cook over medium heat until browned. Turn the bones occasionally.
3. Add the wine and continue cooking until the wine evaporates. Add the cup of water, lower the heat, cover the skillet, and cook 1 hour. Add more water, if necessary.
4. Five minutes before serving, add the parsley, garlic, lemon peel, and anchovy. Cook 2 minutes longer, turning the bones over once.
5. Place the bones on a serving dish. Add the stock and butter to the pan gravy, mix well until the sauce thickens, and pour it over the bones.

Serves 4

Beef Braciole in Tomato Sauce

||||||||

Rolled Stuffed Beef

You'd better make a couple—this will be a big favorite!

1 ½ pounds flank, skirt, or top of the round steak
2 garlic cloves, finely chopped
¼ cup chopped fresh parsley
¼ cup freshly grated Parmesan cheese
½ teaspoon salt

⅛ teaspoon freshly ground black pepper
⅓ cup olive oil
2½ cups canned peeled and crushed tomatoes
*pinch of dried basil, red pepper flakes, mint, and
    oregano*
salt and freshly ground black pepper to taste

1. Lay the meat out flat on a smooth working surface. Flatten it to ½-inch thickness, pounding it lightly with the dull edge of a meat cleaver, or use a meat mallet. Keep the meat in one piece.
2. Cover the steak with the garlic, parsley, cheese, salt, and pepper.
3. Roll up the steak, jellyroll fashion, and tie it securely with cotton string or several toothpicks.
4. Heat the oil in a large heavy skillet and brown the meat thoroughly on all sides. This should take 10 minutes.
5. Add the tomatoes and seasonings to the browned *braciole*. Cover the skillet. Simmer the meat for about 1 hour or until it is tender. Do not overcook, or it will fall apart.
6. When the meat is ready, place it on a large serving platter, cut the string, slice, and serve with the sauce poured over it. This may be accompanied by cooked pasta.

   NOTE: This can be made in advance and reheated. It can be refrigerated for 3 to 5 days, and it freezes well if it is covered with the sauce.

Serves 4

Meatballs

▌▌▌▌▌▌▌▌

Try making meatballs smaller than 1 inch in diameter and serving them with your favorite sauce. They make an excellent appetizer for a buffet dinner.

1 pound ground meat (½ beef, ½ pork)
3 medium eggs

³/₄ cup bread crumbs, or enough to hold mixture together
¹/₄ cup chopped fresh parsley
¹/₄ cup freshly grated Parmesan or Romano cheese
1 large garlic clove, finely chopped
salt and pepper to taste

1. Combine all the ingredients in a large bowl. Toss gently with your hands until the meat has become thoroughly blended with all the seasonings. The mixture should be fairly moist.
2. To form the meatballs, wet your hands in a small bowl of lukewarm water and then pick up about ¹/₃ cup of the meatball mixture. Roll it in the palm of your hands to form a smooth ball about 1 inch in diameter.
3. Drop the meatballs directly into your basic tomato sauce recipe. Or, if you prefer a crusty meatball, fry in approximately 3 tablespoons of olive oil on medium heat for about 5 minutes, turning to brown evenly. Then drop them into gently boiling tomato sauce as they are browned. Meatballs take 20 minutes to cook well. (Remember to scrape the bottom of the skillet and pour any crusty meat particles into the meat sauce.)

Yield: 15–18 medium meatballs or
40–45 tiny meatballs

Italian Beef Stew

IIIIIII

Experiment with different kinds of wine in this stew. Burgundy will keep it on the sweet side, while a dry white wine will keep it light.

2 pounds cubed lean beef
flour
4 tablespoons olive oil

¼ cup butter
2 ounces salt pork, diced into small pieces
3 large onions, thickly sliced
salt and freshly ground black pepper to taste
3 garlic cloves, minced
10 sprigs parsley, leaves only, chopped
1 bay leaf, crumbled
½ teaspoon dried basil
pinch of dried thyme and marjoram
½ cup wine
3 large potatoes, cut in chunks
3 celery stalks, sliced
3 or 4 carrots, sliced in chunks
2 medium-size fresh tomatoes, diced, or
* 1 14-ounce can plum tomatoes*
½ pound mushrooms, thinly sliced
½ cup hot water

1. Dredge the meat in flour. Shake off the excess.
2. Heat the olive oil, butter, and salt pork in a heavy pot or Dutch oven. Remove the salt pork when it is slightly browned. Add the onions, beef, salt, and pepper. Cook for 10 minutes, stirring often.
3. Add the garlic, chopped parsley, bay leaf, basil, thyme, and marjoram. Let the mixture heat thoroughly. Sprinkle the wine into the pot. Stir and simmer, covered, for 10 minutes.
4. Add the potatoes, celery, carrots, tomatoes, and mushrooms. Stir and cook for 10 minutes longer.
5. Add the hot water, cover, and simmer for 40 minutes, stirring at least twice to prevent sticking.
6. Uncover the stew and simmer 10 minutes more or until the meat is tender. Taste for salt and pepper and add more if needed.

NOTE: This stew refrigerates well for several days.

Serves 4–6

My Mother's Trippa

IIIIIIII

My Mother's Tripe

When people refer to "Italian Soul Food," this has to be one of the things they have in mind. Tripe is both a peasant's dish and a delicacy. It is a Saturday afternoon favorite in local Italian neighborhood restaurants. Honeycomb tripe can be purchased at the local butcher and often at the supermarket as well.

> *3 pounds honeycomb tripe*
> *1/2 cup olive oil*
> *1 garlic clove, chopped*
> *1/2 large onion, chopped*
> *1 tablespoon dried red pepper flakes*
> *3 bay leaves*
> *dash Tabasco*
> *3 ounces canned tomato paste*
> *1 28-ounce can peeled and crushed tomatoes*
> *salt and pepper to taste*
> *1/2 cup freshly grated Parmesan cheese, plus more*
>   *for serving*
> *freshly chopped parsley*

1. Rinse the tripe under cold running water and scrub it with salt until it is white and clean.
2. Place the tripe in a deep pot filled with about 5 quarts of cold water. Cover and let it come to a soft boil. Continue cooking for about 1 hour or until tender. Drain and rinse under cold water until it is cool enough to handle. Cut it into pieces about 3 inches long and 1 inch wide. Reserve.
3. Heat the oil in a large pot. Saute the chopped garlic, onion, red pepper flakes, bay leaves, and Tabasco. Add the tomato paste and stir briskly. Add the can of tomatoes, salt, and pepper. Stir constantly until all the ingredients are blended and gently boiling.

4. Add the tripe and simmer, covered, for about ½ hour.
5. Now add the grated cheese and parsley. Simmer again for about 15 more minutes. Remove the bay leaves. Shut off the heat and wait about ½ hour before serving.
6. Serve with plenty of grated cheese and additional salt and pepper.

    NOTE: This can be prepared a day or two ahead of serving. It refrigerates well and can be frozen.

Serves 6

Lamb Stew

IIIIIII

Nothing can beat a bowl of stew. It is warm and nourishing and full of love.

> *3 pounds lamb chunks*
> *flour*
> *½ cup oil*
> *2 garlic cloves, crushed*
> *4 carrots, thickly sliced*
> *3 or 4 celery stalks, sliced*
> *3 large onions, sliced*
> *2 large potatoes, thickly sliced*
> *1 heaping tablespoon tomato paste*
> *1 14-ounce can whole tomatoes, or 2 cups*
>   *Marinara Sauce (see page 30)*
> *salt and pepper to taste*
> *pinch of dried red pepper flakes, mint, oregano,*
>   *and basil*
> *1 cup dry white wine*

1. Put the meat in a large bowl and sprinkle with flour, turning often until all sides are coated. Set aside.
2. Put the oil and garlic in a large heavy pot. Saute on low

heat for about 20 minutes so that the oil absorbs all the flavor of the garlic without burning.

3. Meanwhile, start cleaning and preparing the vegetables. Reserve.

4. After the garlic has been cooking for 20 minutes, remove it from the oil. Raise the heat to high and fry the lamb and onions until they are well browned, turning often.

5. Lower the heat to medium. Add the tomato paste and stir well. Now add the tomatoes or Marinara Sauce and seasonings. Stir until mixed thoroughly. Saute for about 5 minutes, turning often.

6. Sprinkle the cup of wine all over and simmer, covered, for 20 minutes. Stir several times during cooking.

7. After 20 minutes, add the carrots, celery, potatoes, and more of the seasonings. Stir well and cover. Cook for another $1/2$ hour or until the meat is tender. Turn off the heat and let the mixture rest (covered) for about 20 minutes.

NOTE: This stew freezes and refrigerates well.

Serves 6-8

IIII Cutting onions with a very sharp knife helps keep your eyes from tearing. **IIII**

Lamb with
White Wine Sauce

IIIIIII

3 pounds leg of lamb, boned and cut in cubes
1/2 cup flour
1 garlic clove, chopped
1 teaspoon dried rosemary
1/4 cup olive oil
salt and pepper to taste
1 cup dry white wine
1 teaspoon tomato paste
1/4 cup warm water
1 cup canned peeled plum tomatoes, squeezed to
    break into small pieces
1 8-ounce can of peas (optional)

1. Put the lamb cubes and flour in a paper bag. Shake the bag to coat the meat evenly with flour.
2. Chop the garlic and rosemary together into tiny bits. Heat the olive oil in a Dutch oven over high heat. Saute the garlic and rosemary until golden.
3. Add the lamb to the Dutch oven. Brown it thoroughly by turning it over and over on all sides. Add salt, a few grinds of pepper, and the wine. Stir gently and cook for about 5 minutes. Reduce the heat to medium.
4. Dilute the tomato paste in the warm water. Add it to the Dutch oven, stir gently, then add the tomatoes. Bring all the ingredients to a soft boil, reduce heat, and simmer 1 hour, stirring occasionally. Remove the stew from the heat.
5. I like to throw a can of peas in the pot after the lamb has completed cooking. Stir gently, cover the pot, and let the stew rest for about 10 minutes.
6. Serve with buttered noodles or garlic bread.

    NOTE: This stew can be made ahead and refrigerated or frozen.

Serves 6

Rabbit Siciliano

IIIIIIII

Chicken can be substituted for the rabbit in this recipe, but since we don't often find a good rabbit recipe, why not give it a try in its authentic version?

> *1 small rabbit (about 3 pounds), cut in small pieces*
> *²/₃ cup olive oil*
> *2 celery stalks, sliced*
> *1 6-ounce jar black, dry-cured, Sicilian olives, pitted and halved*
> *2 garlic cloves, chopped*
> *¹/₄ teaspoon dried oregano*
> *pinch of dried red pepper flakes*
> *freshly ground black pepper to taste*
> *1 teaspoon salt*
> *1 teaspoon capers in water, drained*
> *¹/₂ cup white vinegar*

1. Wash the rabbit well. Soak it in cold salted water for several hours. Dry with paper towels and reserve.
2. Heat the oil in a large heavy skillet and saute the sliced celery for 5 minutes. Remove the celery from the pan and reserve.
3. Raise the heat and fry the rabbit a few pieces at a time until nicely browned.
4. Lower the heat to medium and add the celery, olives, garlic, seasonings, and capers. Stir gently until the rabbit and seasonings are well blended. Sprinkle with the vinegar, and simmer, covered, for about ¹/₂ hour or until the rabbit is tender. Add more of the above seasonings if needed.
5. Remove the pan from the heat and let it rest, covered, for about 10 minutes to combine flavors. Serve with noodles and a salad.

   NOTE: This can be refrigerated for several days.

Serves 4

Olga's Rabbit Cacciatore

||||||||

When I was a child, my grandfather would come over often and request that my mother prepare this recipe. Since he always asked for it in Italian, my brothers, sisters and I always thought we were eating chicken, and my mother didn't tell us any differently since she thought we might be a little sensitive to eating a rabbit. We used to get a bunny each Easter and raise it as our pet. When it became grown we were told it had to be given away. Little did we know it was to become a Sunday dinner. Only in later years did we find out how lucky we were to have such delicacies as Rabbit Cacciatore as part of our ethnic tradition.

> 1 small rabbit (about 3 pounds), cut in small
>   pieces
> 2/3 cup olive oil
> 2 large green peppers, sliced
> 3 medium onions, sliced lengthwise
> 1/2 pound button mushrooms, cut in chunks
> 6 garlic cloves, halved
> salt and pepper to taste
> 3 red, ripe tomatoes, peeled and chopped
> dried red pepper flakes to taste
> 1 6-ounce can small peas (reserve juice)

1. Wash the rabbit well and soak it in cold salted water for several hours. Dry with paper towels and reserve.
2. Put the oil in a large heavy skillet and saute the peppers until tender. Remove them from the oil and set aside. Saute the onions until tender and remove them from the oil. Add to the peppers. Saute the mushrooms and 3 garlic cloves until slightly browned. Add to the peppers and onions.
3. Now put the rabbit and the remaining garlic cloves in the skillet and fry until browned. Salt and pepper the meat. Add the tomatoes, stirring gently. Cover.
4. Let the rabbit boil slightly to dry out any remaining water. Add red pepper flakes, more salt and pepper, and

other seasonings, if desired. If the mixture becomes too dry, add juice from the can of peas.

5. Remove the cover after 20 minutes and add the pepper and onion mixture. Let simmer 10 minutes, then add the peas. Remove the skillet from the heat and let rest for a few minutes to allow flavors to combine.

NOTE: This dish may be refrigerated for a couple of days.

Serves 4

Italian Sausages, Vinegar Peppers, and Potatoes

IIIIIIII

Pork chops may be substituted for the sausages in this recipe.

> *2 pounds sweet, all-pork Italian sausages*
> *¼ cup olive oil*
> *6 large potatoes, peeled, thickly sliced, and wiped dry*
> *6–8 spicy or hot vinegar peppers*
> *salt and pepper to taste*

1. In a large heavy skillet, over medium heat, fry the sausages in hot oil until well browned. Pierce them gently with a fork as they cook. Using a slotted spoon, transfer the sausages to a large platter.
2. In the same skillet, on high heat, add the clean, dried potatoes. (To prevent the potatoes from sticking, add a little salt to hot oil.) Cook until crispy, turning them often with a spatula.
3. Keep the heat on high and add the cooked sausages, stirring gently.
4. When all the ingredients are well heated, add the vinegar peppers, one at a time. Tear them into bite-size pieces over the skillet, allowing the juices to fall over the sausages and potatoes. Toss gently. The pepper

juices will cause the mixture to steam, so be careful. Saute for about 3 minutes and add more salt if needed.

5. Remove the skillet from the heat and let rest for 5 minutes. Serve with Italian bread and a salad.

NOTE: If you are on a busy schedule, fry the sausages and prepare all of the ingredients early in the day. Keep the sliced, uncooked potatoes in water, however, or they will brown. Then assemble and cook the dish just prior to serving. It is best that it be eaten the same day as it is prepared because the potatoes, in particular, will not taste the same after refrigeration.

Serves 4

Polla al Cacciatore
IIIIIII
Chicken Cacciatore

¾ cup olive oil
3 cloves garlic, crushed
2 pounds boneless, skinless chicken breasts,
*   washed, dried, and cut into strips*
salt and pepper to taste
2 green peppers, cut into strips
2 red peppers, cup into strips
4 medium onions, sliced thick
1 12-ounce can plum tomatoes
½ teaspoon red pepper flakes (optional)
1 cup whole button mushrooms or sliced larger
*   mushrooms*
chopped fresh parsley

1. Using a large heavy skillet with cover, add the olive oil and crushed garlic and saute until garlic is golden brown. Remove the garlic.
2. When the oil is fairly hot, add the chicken pieces and saute until the chicken is nicely browned, turning as needed, adding salt and pepper to taste. Cover the chicken and let it simmer over a low flame until it is tender, about 5 minutes.

3. Add the sliced peppers and onions; cook until they are tender but not limp.
4. Using a medium-high heat, add the tomatoes with their juices. Season to taste, adding red pepper flakes if desired.
5. When the tomatoes have cooked to form a sauce consistency, add the mushrooms and sprinkle with fresh parsley. Toss the mixture in the pan to allow the flavors to blend. Cover and let rest ½ hour before serving. Serve at room temperature, or reheat if preferred.

NOTE: This may be eaten as a main course or alongside cooked spaghetti with crusty Italian bread.

Serves 4–6

Chicken Cacciatore, Italian-Stew Style

IIIIIII

2 chickens washed, dried, and cut into pieces
   (remove skin if desired)
2 cloves garlic, chopped
1 teaspoon salt
1 teaspoon freshly ground pepper
1 teaspoon red pepper flakes (optional)
2 stalks celery, cut into small pieces
1 medium-size onion, sliced
½ cup chopped fresh parsley
1 large green pepper, sliced
3 medium-size tomatoes, cut into small pieces
1 15-ounce can tomato sauce
¼ cup tomato paste mixed with ½ cup
   white wine

1. Brown the chickens well in 1½ inches of hot olive oil in a large skillet (about 2 inches deep) using medium heat.
2. Add the garlic and saute for 1 minute. Season with salt and pepper and red pepper flakes.

3. Add the celery, onion, parsley, green pepper, and tomatoes. Cook, reducing heat a little, until the vegetables are tender.
4. Add the tomato sauce and tomato paste. Put a cover on the skillet and cook on low heat for about 30 minutes or less, turning once or twice. Let the mixture rest for 15 minutes to allow flavors to blend.

   NOTE: This makes a complete meal when served with a salad and crusty bread.

Serves 8

Chicken Limone

IIIIIIII

This dish is best made right before serving. Be sure to have all your ingredients prepared and on hand. As with most breast of chicken dishes, veal may be substituted for the chicken.

> *6 boneless chicken breasts*
> *2 eggs*
> *¼ cup milk*
> *1 cup flour*
> *¼ cup butter*
> *¼ cup olive oil*
> *4 tablespoons unsalted butter*
> *2 lemons*
> *salt and pepper to taste*
> *1 tablespoon chopped fresh parsley*

1. Slice the chicken breasts into very thin medallions (or buy small chicken cutlets).
2. In a large bowl, beat the eggs with the milk. Put the flour on a shallow plate.
3. Heat the ¼ cup of butter and oil in a heavy skillet on medium temperature. At the same time, dredge the chicken in the flour, then dip it quickly in the egg wash.

4. Saute the chicken for a few minutes on each side until golden brown.
5. Transfer the chicken to a serving platter and keep warm. Pour off any oils that remain in the skillet.
6. Add the 4 tablespoons of unsalted butter to the skillet. With a wooden spoon, loosen all the particles on the bottom of the pan.
7. Raise the heat under the skillet. Squeeze the juice of one lemon into the skillet. Add salt, pepper, and chopped parsley.
8. Slice the second lemon. Overlap the chicken and the lemon slices on the serving platter. Pour the sauce on top and serve immediately with hot buttered linguine or noodles.

Serves 6

Chicken Braciolittini with Mushroom and Wine Sauce

IIIIIIII

This is a favorite of all my recipes. It is elegant, easy to prepare, and certainly has eye appeal. Serve it with asparagus and fresh homemade buttered noodles and you will be sure to please almost everyone.

> *6 large boneless chicken breasts*
> *1 large garlic clove*
> *freshly ground black pepper*
> *¹/₄ cup freshly grated Parmesan or Romano cheese*
> *¹/₂ pound shredded mozzarella or fontina cheese*
> *¹/₄ bunch fresh parsley, chopped (reserve 1*
>   *tablespoon for garnish)*
> *6 thin slices prosciutto*
> *¹/₄ cup oil*
> *¹/₄ cup margarine*
> *¹/₂ cup butter*

¹/₂ cut Madeira or Marsala wine
*¹/₂ pound whole button mushrooms or thinly
sliced mushrooms*

1. Have butcher pound the meat slightly to break the tendons, or use the flat side of a heavy meat cleaver to do so yourself.
2. Lay the flat pieces of chicken on a smooth clean surface. Using a garlic press, squeeze the garlic clove. With your fingertips, transfer these particles to the cutlet pieces. Sprinkle black pepper, grated cheese, shredded cheese, and parsley all over the chicken. Cover each breast with a slice of prosciutto. Roll each breast jellyroll style, carefully tucking in all loose ends. Secure with toothpicks.
3. Heat the oil and margarine in a large skillet over medium heat. Add the chicken breasts and brown well all over. With a slotted spoon, transfer the chicken to a baking pan. Bake for 20 minutes in a preheated 350-degree oven or until the chicken is cooked through.
4. Drain the fat from the skillet. Put the ¹/₂ cup of butter in the skillet. As it melts, scrape up all the browned particles at the bottom of the pan to mix with the butter.
5. Raise the heat to high. Pour in the wine, stirring well. Add the mushrooms and cook 1 more minute. If the sauce appears too thin, sprinkle in some flour and let the sauce cook until it reaches your desired thickness.
6. Remove the chicken from the oven and place on a heated serving platter. Pour the sauce on top. Sprinkle with the reserved tablespoon of chopped parsley and serve.

   NOTE: This dish may be refrigerated for 2 or 3 days.

Serves 6

Boneless Chicken Breasts with Broccoli

IIIIIIII

A really quick, easy, and delicious meal.

3 large boneless chicken breasts
1 bunch broccoli
1/2 cup olive oil
1 garlic clove, chopped
1 shallot clove, chopped
salt and pepper to taste
1/2 pound ziti
2 tablespoons unsalted butter
1/2 cup freshly grated Parmesan cheese

1. Cut the chicken breasts into cubes. Cut the broccoli into flowerets. (Save the stems for another use, such as a broccoli sauce for pasta.)
2. Heat 1/4 cup oil in a large skillet over medium heat. Saute the chicken with the garlic, shallot, salt, and pepper until lightly browned. Using a slotted spoon, transfer the chicken to a large platter. Discard the drippings and wipe out the pan.
3. Add the remaining 1/4 cup of oil to the pan. Warm the oil and then add the broccoli flowerets. Stir-fry for about 5 minutes. Add the chicken, toss lightly, and remove from heat.
4. Meanwhile, cook the ziti according to package directions. Drain, but do not rinse.
5. Toss the ziti with the butter. Add to the chicken and broccoli and toss gently. Sprinkle with the grated Parmesan cheese and more salt and pepper to taste. Serve.

NOTE: If you wish, this dish can be refrigerated for 2 or 3 days and then reheated gently before serving.

Serves 4

Pollastro in Tecia

IIIIIII

Casserole Chicken

Hot pasta will nicely complement this chicken dish. If time is a concern, cook the casserole early in the day, refrigerate it, and reheat just before serving.

> *1 chicken (approximately 2 1/2 pounds)*
> *1 1/2 tablespoons olive oil*
> *4 tablespoons butter*
> *1 medium onion, finely chopped*
> *1 carrot, finely chopped*
> *1 celery stalk, sliced*
> *1 14-ounce can Italian peeled tomatoes, squeezed*
>   *to break into small pieces*
> *1/2 cup dry white wine*
> *2 whole cloves*
> *pinch of ground cinnamon*
> *1 pound whole button mushrooms*
> *salt and pepper to taste*

1. Wash and wipe the chicken and cut it into bite-size pieces using a butcher's knife.
2. Heat the oil and butter in a fairly large casserole dish that can be safely placed on a burner. Over medium heat, saute the onion, carrot, and celery. Add the cut-up chicken and fry until it is golden brown.
3. Raise the heat to high and add the tomatoes. Cook for 5 minutes, stirring frequently. Add the white wine and let the mixture come to a boil, stirring well. Now add the cloves and cinnamon and lower the heat. Continue cooking until the chicken is tender, about 1/2 hour, stirring once or twice.
4. Fifteen minutes before the chicken is cooked add the whole mushrooms. Season with salt and pepper.
5. Let rest for about 20 minutes before serving.

Serves 6

Shellfish and Fish Dishes

||||||||

Shrimp Scampi Aglio e Olio

IIIIIII

Fried Shrimp in Olive Oil Sauce

This recipe, served with a salad, your favorite wine, and plenty of bread, will bring smiles to a lot of faces. It works well as an appetizer or a main course.

3 garlic cloves, chopped
pinch of dried tarragon and red pepper flakes
½ cup olive oil (or more if additional sauce is
  desired)
1 pound medium shrimp, unpeeled
salt and freshly ground black pepper to taste
¼ cup chopped fresh parsley

1. In a heavy skillet, on low heat, saute the garlic, tarragon, and red pepper flakes in the olive oil. Simmer for a couple of minutes.
2. Raise the heat to high. When the oil is red hot, add the shrimp. Toss them gently until they turn pink.
3. Remove the skillet from the heat, and add salt, pepper, and parsley. Serve immediately with plenty of Italian bread to sop up the juices.

   NOTE: Our local fishermen say that leaving the shell on the shrimp while you cook them will help them stay juicy and prevent shrinking.

Serves 2–3

Baked Stuffed Shrimp Italiano

██████

Try this stuffing with lobsters or clams. It is excellent!

1 1/2 pounds large shrimp, unpeeled
1/2 pound coarse bread crumbs
1/4 pound salted crackers, crumbled
3 ounces canned crabmeat (optional)
1/2 cup freshly grated Parmesan cheese
1/2 cup chopped fresh parsley
4 tablespoons butter, melted
1/4 cup lemon juice
few drops of Tabasco
1 garlic clove, chopped
pinch of dried tarragon
salt and freshly ground black pepper to taste
paprika (optional)
olive oil
lemon slices for garnish

1. Leave the shell on the shrimp. Remove all tentacles. Lay each shrimp flat on the counter and devein. Slice and spread open butterfly-style.
2. In a large bowl, mix the bread crumbs, crackers, crabmeat (optional), grated cheese, parsley, melted butter, lemon juice, Tabasco, garlic, and tarragon. Add salt and pepper to taste.
3. Stuff each shrimp until it is well packed. Place the stuffed shrimp on a cookie sheet, each one nestled into another, in a half-moon curve, so the stuffing will stay secure. Sprinkle with paprika, if desired.
4. Drizzle olive oil lightly over the shrimp. Bake the shrimp in a preheated 400-degree oven on the middle rack for about 20 minutes, or until golden brown.
5. Serve with plenty of lemon slices.

Serves 4–6

Cioppino

IIIIIII

This is not exactly a soup, and not exactly a stew. It is a combination of flavors that are light and nutritious.

1/3 cup olive or vegetable oil
3 garlic cloves, chopped
1 1/4 cups chopped onion
3/4 cup sliced scallions
1/2 cup chopped green pepper
1 6-ounce can tomato paste
1 28-ounce can plum tomatoes
1/2 bunch parsley, chopped
1 teaspoon dried oregano
1 teaspoon dried basil
1 teaspoon dried red pepper flakes
1 teaspoon dried tarragon
salt and pepper to taste
1 1/4 cups Burgundy wine
1 11 1/2-ounce jar whole clams, undrained
1 1/2 pounds haddock, sole, or halibut (no bones)
1 1/2 pounds medium-size shrimp, unpeeled
3 6 1/2-ounce cans crabmeat, drained

1. Heat the oil in a 6-quart kettle. Saute the garlic, onions, scallions, and green peppers until tender (about 10 minutes), stirring often.
2. Add the tomato paste and stir until well blended. Add the can of tomatoes, including the juice. Stir gently until the mixture comes to a boil. Add salt and pepper to taste.
3. Simmer for about 5 minutes, then add the wine. Simmer for 10 minutes, and then add the clams, fish of your choice, shrimp, and crabmeat. (You may cut the fish into chunks if the pieces are too large but they are likely to break apart in the cooking process.) At this point you may need more salt and pepper.
4. Simmer, covered, for about 15 minutes, then uncovered for 15 minutes more.

5. Remove the kettle from the heat and let it rest for about 10 minutes.
6. Serve in large bowls, accompanied by garlic bread and salad. Put a large empty bowl in the middle of the table to receive the shells. Have plenty of napkins available.

NOTE: Cioppino can be refrigerated, but it is best served the same day.

Serves 6

Quick Seafood Diavolo

A hot and spicy fish medley. Serve it proudly, for you will enjoy the enthusiasm of the whole family. It is best served the day it is made.

> *¹/₂ cup olive oil*
> *1 garlic clove, chopped*
> *1 bunch scallions, chopped*
> *pinch of dried red pepper flakes and oregano*
> *a few drops of Tabasco*
> *¹/₄ pound mushrooms, chopped*
> *2 cups canned tomatoes, or 3 peeled tomatoes, chopped, with juices*
> *¹/₄ cup dry white wine*
> *12 littleneck clams, scrubbed clean*
> *12 mussels, scrubbed clean and debearded*
> *6 fresh shrimp, or 1 can any size shrimp*
> *¹/₂ pound baby scallops, or large scallops, quartered*
> *¹/₂ cup bottled clam juice*
> *salt and pepper to taste*
> *¹/₂ pound of any firm white fish (sole, haddock, etc.)*
> *1 pound linguine or thin spaghetti*
> *2 tablespoons butter or margarine*
> *chopped fresh parsley*

1. Heat the oil in a large kettle over medium heat. Add the garlic, scallions, red pepper flakes, oregano, Tabasco, and mushrooms.
2. When the mixture starts to brown, add the tomatoes and their juices. Simmer for 2 minutes. Raise the heat to high. Add the white wine and let the sauce come to a boil. Add the clams, mussels, shrimp, scallops, and clam juice. Sprinkle with salt and pepper to taste.
3. Cook, covered, on medium-low heat until the clams start to open. At this point, add the white fish. Salt and pepper again to taste, if desired. Cover again and cook for 3 minutes.
4. Meanwhile, cook linguine or thin spaghetti according to package directions. Drain well and toss with the butter. Put onto a large serving platter.
5. Cover the pasta with half of the sauce. Sprinkle with parsley. Place the shellfish around the outside of the platter. Pour the remaining sauce into a serving bowl for use by the family as desired.

Serves 4–6

Scallops Marinara
IIIIIIII

½ cup butter or margarine
1 pound fresh sea scallops
2 cloves garlic, chopped
3 scallions, chopped
1 small onion, chopped
1 16-ounce can whole tomatoes, chopped
   (reserve juice)
¼ pound fresh button mushrooms, quartered
¼ cup dry white wine
1 tablespoon lemon juice
salt and freshly ground pepper to taste
pinch tarragon
¼ cup chopped fresh parsley

1. In a large heavy skillet, melt the butter or margarine. Add the scallops, garlic, scallions, and onion. Saute for about 3 minutes, stirring gently.
2. Add the tomatoes and mushrooms and saute about 2 minutes.
3. Add the wine and lemon juice, salt, pepper, and tarragon. Cook briskly on medium-high heat for about 2 to 3 minutes.
4. Add the reserved tomato juice and cook on high heat for about 5 minutes. Add the parsley and serve immediately. You may wish to serve spaghetti or linguine on the side.

Serves 2–3

Italian-Style Steamed Mussels

IIIIIIII

Serve these mussels as an appetizer.

> *3 quarts mussels*
> *12 shallots, thinly sliced*
> *1 onion, thinly sliced*
> *2 tablespoons olive oil*
> *2 tablespoons unsalted butter*
> *4 garlic cloves, chopped*
> *¹/₂ cup bottled clam juice*
> *¹/₂ cup dry white wine*
> *1 bay leaf*
> *3 heaping tablespoons chopped Italian parsley*
> *1 teaspoon dried thyme*
> *1 teaspoon freshly ground black pepper*

1. Clean the mussels carefully and pull off the beards. Discard any mussels with open shells. Keep refrigerated until ready to use.

2. In a heavy pot large enough to hold the mussels, saute the shallots and onions in the oil and butter over low heat until translucent, not brown. Add the garlic during the last 2 minutes of sauteing.
3. Add the clam juice, white wine, bay leaf, parsley, thyme, and pepper. Cook, covered, over low heat, 10 to 15 minutes.
4. Raise the heat and add the mussels. Cook, covered, just until all the shells are opened. Discard any unopened mussels. Remove the bay leaf.
5. Serve hot in soup bowls, accompanied by crusty Italian bread. Provide extra plates for the empty shells.

Serves 6–8

Quick Mussels Marinara

IIIIIIII

This is an appealing appetizer in which the fish and tomatoes combine to produce a light, traditional flavor.

> *4 quarts mussels*
> *olive oil (enough to cover the bottom of the pan)*
> *2 garlic cloves, finely chopped*
> *¹/₄ teaspoon dried oregano*
> *1 tablespoon dried basil (use fresh if available)*
> *¹/₄ teaspoon dried tarragon*
> *¹/₄ teaspoon dried red pepper flakes*
> *2 teaspoons chopped fresh parsley*
> *1 14-ounce can peeled and crushed tomatoes*
> *salt and pepper to taste*
> *1 cup dry white wine*

1. Scrub the mussels well. Scrape off the beards, using your fingers or a rough brush. Rinse under cold running

water and drain. Discard any mussels with shells that remain open when tapped. Keep the mussels refrigerated until ready to use.

2. In a pot large enough to hold the mussels, combine the olive oil, garlic, oregano, basil, tarragon, red pepper, and parsley. Saute on low heat for about 5 minutes.

3. Add the tomatoes, salt, and pepper. Let the mixture come to a gentle boil, and cook on low heat for about 15 minutes to blend the flavors. Add the wine and mussels. Cover and cook 5 to 8 minutes, shaking the pan so the mussels cook evenly. Discard any unopened mussels.

4. Serve in heated soup bowls with crusty Italian bread or pour over linguine.

Serves 4–6

Clam and Mussel Stew

IIIIIII

A perfect summer appetizer, and equally good as a light meal.

> 1 pound mussels
> 1 pound small clams
> 2 tablespoons olive oil
> 1/2 large onion, chopped
> 1 garlic clove, chopped
> 1 1/2 pounds ripe tomatoes, peeled, seeded, and chopped
> 1/2 cup dry white wine
> 1/4 teaspoon dried thyme
> 1 bay leaf
> freshly ground black pepper to taste
> 1/4 cup water
> 1 tablespoon chopped fresh parsley

1. Scrub the mussels and clams well. Scrape off the beards on the mussels, using your fingers or a rough brush.

Rinse under cold running water and drain. Discard any mussels or clams with shells that do not close when tapped.

2. Heat the olive oil in a heavy frying pan. Add the onion and cook over low heat, stirring often, until soft, but not brown.

3. Stir in the garlic and cook for half a minute. Add the tomatoes and stir for 2 minutes over medium-high heat. Add the wine, thyme, bay leaf, and pepper. Cook for 12 to 15 minutes or until thick, stirring often. Discard the bay leaf.

4. Meanwhile, put the mussels in a large saucepan. Cover and cook over high heat for about 5 minutes or until the mussels open. Shake the pan often as the mussels cook. Remove the mussels with a slotted spoon; discard any that do not open.

5. Carefully pour the mussel liquid into a bowl, trying to eliminate any sand particles. Discard the sandy water. If the water in the bowl is still sandy, let it rest for a few minutes, then carefully pour it into another bowl, leaving the sand behind.

6. Put the clams in the saucepan with the ¼ cup of water. Cover and cook over medium-high heat, shaking the pan often until the clams open. Remove the clams with a slotted spoon; discard any that do not open. Reserve the liquid, leaving the sand behind as you did with the mussels.

7. Gradually add half the mussel liquid and half the clam liquid to the tomato mixture.

8. Taste; if you desire more salt, add more mussel and clam liquid. Heat the mixture again until slightly thickened but not dry. Add the mussels and clams in their shells. Cover and heat for a few minutes.

9. Serve in bowls with a sprinkle of chopped parsley.

Serves 2–3

Mr. Ciani's Baked Stuffed Clams

IIIIIIII

Mr. Ciani is a 99-year-old veteran in the kitchen, to which he would invite his entire family and cook and serve them a nine-course meal. Of course, he had someone come in afterward to clean up the mess!

> *12 large clams*
> *1 cup Italian-style dry bread crumbs*
> *2 garlic cloves, chopped*
> *1 tablespoon finely chopped fresh parsley*
> *salt and pepper to taste*
> *olive oil (just enough to cover the bottom of the pan)*
> *1/2 cup freshly grated Parmesan cheese*
> *lemon wedges for garnish*

1. Scrub the clams thoroughly. Open them carefully and pour the juices into a bowl. Chop the clams into small pieces and add to the juices. Reserve 12 shells on a baking sheet.
2. Saute the bread crumbs, garlic, parsley, salt, and pepper in the olive oil for about 2 minutes, stirring constantly. You may add more oil if the mixture seems too dry. When the garlic begins to brown, remove the pan from the heat.
3. Add this mixture to the clams and juices, and toss lightly.
4. Spoon the mixture into the clam shells until they are filled. Sprinkle lightly with the Parmesan cheese.
5. Bake the clams in a preheated 375-degree oven for 25–30 minutes or until a crust forms on the stuffing.
6. Serve with lemon wedges.

   NOTE: If Mr. Ciani does not mind my meddling, I like to add a dash or two of Tabasco sauce in the stuffing.

Serves 6

Calamari con Vino

IIIIIII

Squid with Wine

2 tablespoons olive oil
2 cloves garlic, chopped
1 pound cleaned squid (cut into 2-inch rings)
¼ cup dry red wine
salt and pepper to taste
1 tablespoon chopped fresh parsley
pinch dried tarragon

To Clean Squid

Separate the head and tentacles from the body. Cut the tentacles apart from the body at the eyes. Discard the head and eyes. Remove the quill and ink sac from the body. Wash out the body; it should be completely empty. Peel off the skin as you wash the body and tentacles under running water. Reserve the tentacles. Drain well.

1. Using a heavy skillet, add the olive oil and lightly brown the garlic.
2. Add the squid and saute 3 minutes, tossing frequently.
3. Add the wine, salt, pepper, parsley, and tarragon. Cook over a high flame until the wine has slightly evaporated.
4. Turn off the heat and let the mixture rest 5 minutes. Serve as an appetizer or over cooked thin spaghetti.

Serves 3–4

Calamari with Fresh Tomatoes Saute

IIIIIIII

This recipe produces a light, delicate meal. It is a tasty, short-cut version of stuffed calamari. As with all calamari dishes, this recipe may be made in advance and refrigerated or frozen.

> *1 1/2 pounds squid, cleaned*
> *1/4 cup plus 1 tablespoon olive oil*
> *1 bunch scallions, chopped*
> *1 shallot, chopped*
> *2 garlic cloves, chopped*
> *1/4 teaspoon dried red pepper flakes*
> *Tabasco*
> *3 1/2 cups peeled and diced fresh tomatoes (seeds discarded)*
> *fresh or dried basil, tarragon, mint, and oregano to taste*
> *salt and freshly ground black pepper to taste*
> *1/2 cup finely chopped fresh parsley*
> *6 black olives, pitted and sliced*
> *lemon wedges for garnish*

1. After the squid has been cleaned as described on page 122, cut the bodies into rings about 1/2 inch wide. Cut the tentacles into bite-size pieces. There should be about 2 1/2 cups. Set aside.
2. Heat the 1/4 cup of oil in a heavy skillet and saute the scallions, shallot, garlic, and red pepper flakes for about 5 minutes on low heat. When the scallions are cooked, raise the heat to high and add the cut squid. Toss lightly and quickly, sprinkling with a dash or two of Tabasco. Cook 2 minutes. With a slotted spoon, take the squid out of the pan and set aside.
3. Dry out all the water from the skillet by boiling rapidly for a few minutes. Then add the tablespoon of olive oil and the fresh tomatoes. Saute the tomatoes, adding

basil, more red pepper flakes, tarragon, mint, oregano, salt, and pepper to taste. Cook 5 minutes.

4. Add the cooked calamari, chopped parsley, and sliced olives. Simmer for 5 minutes, adding more seasonings if needed. Let the mixture rest for 10 minutes so the flavors can meld. Serve with lemon wedges, alone or with spaghetti.

Serves 4

Stewed Squid

▌▌▌▌▌▌▌

This is quick and easy, requiring about half an hour to prepare.

> 2 pounds squid
> 1/4 cup olive oil
> 2 garlic cloves, chopped
> 1 cup canned plum tomatoes, undrained
> pinch of dried tarragon, thyme, and red pepper
>   flakes
> salt and freshly ground black pepper to taste
> 1/2 cup white wine

1. Clean the squid as described on page 122. Cut the bodies into small pieces or in half. Leave the tentacles whole.
2. Heat the olive oil in a saucepan and brown the garlic.
3. Add the tomatoes, thoroughly mashing them with a fork. Add tarragon, thyme, red pepper flakes, salt, and pepper to taste. Cook for 10 minutes on medium heat, stirring often with a wooden spoon.
4. Add the white wine and the squid and boil rapidly over high heat for 3 minutes, stirring often. Lower the heat and cook, uncovered, until tender (about 10 to 20 minutes). Taste and add more salt and pepper if necessary.
5. Serve in soup bowls with lots of garlic bread.

Serves 4

Lobster Bodies in Tomato Sauce

IIIIIII

8–10 lobster bodies
¾ cup olive oil
1 medium onion
2 cloves garlic
2 cloves shallots
pinch each of
*   red pepper flakes*
*   dried tarragon flakes*
*   chopped fresh parsley*
*   dried basil*
1 can chopped mushrooms (reserve liquid)
2 dashes Tabasco
salt and pepper to taste
1 6-ounce can tomato paste
1 28-ounce can crushed tomatoes

1. In a pan large enough to fit the lobsters and tomatoes, add the oil and saute the onion, garlic, shallots, red pepper flakes, tarragon, parsley, and basil, using medium heat. Do not let burn.
2. Add the chopped mushrooms and Tabasco and fry for 5 minutes, turning often.
3. Add the tomato paste and blend well. Add the crushed tomatoes and stir until blended with the tomato paste and oil. Add the salt and pepper and another pinch of seasonings, stirring well.
4. When the sauce starts to slightly boil, add the mushroom liquid and enough water or clam juice to equal ½ can of the tomatoes. Let it come to a boil.
5. Add the lobsters and turn with the sauce. Let the mixture come to another boil, stirring often. Add more salt and pepper if needed.
6. Simmer uncovered for ½ hour, turning the lobsters 4 to 5 times during the cooking period. Serve over 1 pound of cooked linguine that has been tossed with butter.

NOTE: A lobster body is the part left after the claws and tail have been removed. Lobster bodies can be purchased at fish markets, sometimes already cooked. Cooked or fresh ones may be used in this recipe. If using fresh, do not remove the tomalley (liver).

Serves 4–6

Tonno and Noodles, Sicilian Style

IIIIIIII

4 tablespoons olive oil
1 clove garlic, slivered
1 8-ounce can whole tomatoes
1 small can peas
1 large can tonno (tuna)
1 small can ripe pitted olives (or ¼ pound pitted dry-cured Sicilian olives), sliced

1. Heat the oil in a heavy skillet and cook the slivered garlic until golden brown.
2. Remove the garlic and add the tomatoes to the oil, cooking over low heat for ½ hour to thicken.
3. Add the peas and flaked tuna and slivers of ripe olives and heat thoroughly. Be careful not to break up the tuna.
4. Serve over cooked noodles and top, if you like, with a little Parmesan cheese.

Serves 2–4

Eels Marinara

IIIIIIII

Serve this dish as an appetizer, or as a main course with pasta and vegetables.

2 pounds fresh eels
⅓ cup olive oil

1 small onion, minced
2 garlic cloves
1 small piece lemon peel
1/8 teaspoon dried sage
2 tablespoons tomato paste, diluted in 1/2 cup
     water
1/2 cup dry white wine
salt and pepper to taste

1. Have the eels cleaned by the fish merchant and the heads removed and discarded. Rinse thoroughly in cold, salted water, and dry. Cut eels into 3-inch pieces.
2. Pour the oil into a large, deep skillet. Add the onion, garlic, lemon peel, and sage. Saute gently until the garlic is golden brown. Discard the garlic.
3. Add the pieces of eel and fry over medium heat for about 5 minutes. Turn often, gently, using a spatula.
4. Add the diluted tomato paste and wine. Simmer, uncovered, for 10 minutes. Add salt and pepper and simmer for 8 to 10 minutes more.
5. When the liquid is almost evaporated, transfer to a warm serving platter.

NOTE: Refrigerates well for 2 or 3 days.

Serves 2–4

Eels with Peas alla Romana

||||||||

1 1/2 pounds fresh small eels
3 tablespoons olive oil
1/2 garlic clove, minced
4 scallions, sliced
1/2 teaspoon salt
1/2 teaspoon black pepper
pinch of dried red pepper flakes
1/2 cup dry white wine
1 tablespoon tomato sauce

2 cups shelled fresh peas
2 tablespoons warm water or fish stock

1. Have the eels cleaned by the fish merchant and the heads removed and discarded. Rinse thoroughly in cold, salted water, and dry. Cut the eels into 3-inch pieces.
2. Pour the oil into a heavy saucepan. Saute the garlic and scallions until slightly browned.
3. Add the eels, salt, black pepper, and red pepper flakes. Cook on medium-high heat until the liquid from the eels has evaporated.
4. Add the wine, tomato sauce, and peas. Mix well. Add the water or stock and lower the heat to medium. Cook, uncovered for 15 to 20 minutes or until the peas are tender. Stir gently a couple of times only. Taste for more salt and pepper.
5. Serve in soup bowls with crusty bread.

   NOTE: This dish refrigerates well.

Serves 4

Fried Small Eels

IIIIIIII

Another Christmas Eve favorite.

3 pounds fresh small eels
1 cup flour
salt and pepper to taste
1 cup olive oil (use more as needed)
1 lemon, quartered, for garnish

1. Have the eels cleaned by the fish merchant and the heads removed and discarded. Rinse thoroughly in cold, salted water and pat dry with paper towels. Cut them into 2-inch pieces.
2. Season the flour with salt and pepper. Put the flour in a brown paper bag. Shake the pieces of eel in the bag, a few at a time, to evenly distribute the flour mixture. Set aside.
3. Heat the olive oil in a medium-size heavy skillet over

medium-high heat. When the oil is hot, add some of the pieces of eel so they can fry uncrowded until brown on both sides. The frying time will be about 15 minutes on each side. Drain on paper towels. Add more oil to the skillet as needed. When all the pieces have been cooked, transfer them to a warm platter.
4. Sprinkle with more salt and pepper, if desired, and serve with lemon quarters.

Serves 4

Haddock alla Pizzaiola

▌▌▌▌▌▌▌

A thick piece of sole may be substituted for the haddock in this recipe.

>*2 pounds haddock fillets*
>*1 pound fresh tomatoes, seed removed, chopped*
>*1 tablespoon chopped fresh parsley*
>*1 large garlic clove, finely chopped*
>*pinch of dried tarragon and mint*
>*salt and freshly ground black pepper to taste*
>*5 tablespoons olive oil*
>*¼ cup freshly grated Parmesan cheese*
>*lemon wedges for garnish (optional)*

1. Place the fish in a buttered baking dish.
2. Mix together the tomatoes, parsley, garlic, seasonings, olive oil, and cheese. Toss gently until well mixed. Spread evenly all over fish fillets.
3. Bake the fish in a preheated 350-degree oven for 20 minutes.
4. Serve very hot with lemon wedges and pan drippings.

Serves 4

Olga's Fish Cakes

IIIIIIII

My mother never had any idea that this recipe would follow her granddaughter to Georgia, where it would become a big hit with all of her friends.

> *3 large boiling potatoes, peeled*
> *3 pounds fish fillets or other skinless pieces*
>   *(pollock, scrod, or any inexpensive boneless fish*
>   *will do)*
> *½ cup freshly grated Parmesan cheese*
> *2 garlic cloves, finely chopped*
> *1 cup chopped fresh parsley*
> *3 eggs*
> *salt and freshly ground black pepper to taste*
> *fresh bread crumbs (enough to hold mixture*
>   *together)*
> *1 cup olive oil*
> *lemon slices, parsley, and tartar sauce (optional)*

1. Cut the potatoes into large cubes and boil for 20 minutes. Drain them thoroughly by shaking the colander well. Then put the potatoes in a large bowl and mash until fluffy.
2. Put the fish in a saucepan (cut it to fit, if necessary). Add water to cover the fish. Boil gently for 5 minutes.
3. Drain the fish and add to the potatoes. Add the grated cheese, garlic, parsley, eggs, salt, and pepper. Gently toss the mixture until well blended.
4. Add bread crumbs a little at a time until the mixture becomes firm to the touch but not dry. Keep the potato-fish mixture light and not laden with crumbs.
5. Bring the mixture to the stove area along with a dish of bread crumbs and a small bowl of water to moisten your hands when rolling the fish cakes. Take a fistful of the fish mixture and roll it into a round ball. When the ball is smooth, gently flatten it to form a patty. Use the water to keep your hands moist (this will prevent the fish cakes from sticking to your palms and help keep a smooth shape). Lightly dust the fish cake with bread

crumbs to dry excess moisture (this will also stop it from sticking to the skillet). Place the fish cake on a large tray and let set for 5 minutes. Repeat with the rest of the mixture.

6. Heat the olive oil in a large heavy skillet on medium-high heat. Gently add the fish cakes to the hot oil without crowding. Fry on both sides until golden brown or until a nice crust forms. Use a spatula to turn the cakes over gently. Transfer to a paper-lined dish to absorb excess oil. Continue until all the mixture has been used.

7. When all the fish cakes have cooked and drained, arrange on a platter with lemon slices, parsley, and tartar sauce. Serve.

Yield: 15 cakes

Mackerel in Tomato Sauce

IIIIIIII

3 pounds mackerel
2 tablespoons olive oil
1 small onion, sliced
1 garlic clove, chopped
1 tablespoon chopped fresh parsley
1 14-ounce can peeled and crushed tomatoes
$1/2$ teaspoon salt
$1/2$ teaspoon black pepper
$1/2$ teaspoon dried red pepper flakes
$1/2$ teaspoon dried basil
$1/2$ teaspoon dried oregano
2 tablespoons water

1. Remove the bones from the mackerel. Cut the mackerel into 4 pieces.
2. Heat the olive oil in a large heavy skillet. Add the onion, garlic, and parsley, and cook until the onions become translucent.
3. Add the tomatoes and seasonings. Cook for 5 minutes on medium heat, stirring often.
4. Add the water and mackerel and cook for 5 more minutes, uncovered. Turn the fish over and cook an addi-

tional 10 minutes.

5. Serve the mackerel in flat plates with the sauce, or serve over spaghetti.

   NOTE: This may be refrigerated for 2–3 days.

Serves 4

Baccalá with Vinegar Peppers

||||||||

This is another of my mother's delicacies. How I enjoy her talents! It should be prepared from several hours to 24 hours in advance to enhance the flavors. Serve with crusty Italian bread as an appetizer or with other main dishes for dinner during Lent.

> *2 pounds dried salt cod (baccalá)*
> *6 large vinegar peppers, hot or sweet*
> *olive oil*
> *salt and freshly ground black pepper to taste*
> *3 large garlic cloves, chopped*
> *chopped fresh parsley*
> *about 10 black, Sicilian, dry-cured olives, pitted*
> *and sliced*

1. Soak the salt cod in enough cold water to cover for 24 hours. Change the water at least six times to remove the salt. Keep refrigerated. When you are ready to cook, drain and rinse well in cold water.

2. Put the fish in a large pot and cover with water. Gently boil on medium heat until the fish is tender. (The fish should not become so soft that it breaks apart in the water.) Rinse under cold running water and drain well.

3. With your fingers, tear the fish into bite-size pieces. Spread them attractively on a large serving platter. Tear the vinegar peppers over the fish, letting the juices fall on the cod.

4. Sprinkle the cod and peppers with a drizzle of olive oil. Use salt only if it is needed, and pepper. Sprinkle the cod and peppers with the chopped garlic, chopped parsley, and black pitted olives. Gently lift the fish with

a spatula to let the other ingredients fall through so everything marinates evenly. Do this several times before serving but try not to disturb the arrangement.

5. Refrigerate, covered, for at least a few hours.

Serves 6–8

Pan-Fried Smelts or Sardines

‖‖‖‖‖

Another quick and easy Lenten delicacy.

*2 pounds fresh whole smelts or sardines (small
    size if possible)*
semolina flour
paprika
salt and pepper
olive oil
*lemon wedges and chopped fresh parsley for
    garnish*

1. Rinse the smelts or sardines under cold water and dry with paper towels.
2. Put 1 cup of flour in a paper bag (adding more as you go along, if needed) along with a sprinkle of paprika, salt, and pepper. Shake 3 or 4 fish at a time in the bag to coat them with flour. When all the fish have been floured, quickly fry in hot olive oil until golden brown. Be careful not to crowd the fish in the pan. Continue until all the fish are used. Drain on paper towels.
3. Serve immediately, garnished with lemon wedges and parsley.

   NOTE: These are best eaten the same day they are made.

Serves 6–8

Vegetables

Roasted Peppers and Onions in Olive Oil

IIIIIIII

Serve as an appetizer, possibly with stuffed mushrooms, or even as a garnish or condiment with a sandwich.

4 red or yellow bell peppers
1/2 cup olive oil
3 small garlic cloves, chopped
1 medium onion, thickly sliced
2 pinches dried oregano
1 tablespoon chopped fresh parsley
salt and freshly ground black pepper to taste

1. Broil the peppers on a broiler pan, at least 4 inches from the heat, turning them often, until the skin is charred and blistered. This will take about 10 minutes. Place the peppers in a paper bag until they are cool enough to handle, about 10 more minutes.
2. Cut the cooled roasted peppers in half, lengthwise. Place on a work surface, with the skin side down. Use a small sharp knife to scrape away seeds and membranes; discard. Turn over, and scrape away and discard stems and skins. Rinse away any traces of charred bits; pat dry with paper towels.
3. Arrange the peppers in a single layer on a large serving platter.
4. Heat the oil in a heavy skillet over low heat until warm. Add the chopped garlic. Saute for about 5 minutes; do not burn. Remove the garlic with a slotted spoon. It may be discarded or put on the peppers (this is a personal decision).
5. Add the onion slices to the warm oil, in a single layer if possible. Saute, turning with a spatula once during cooking, until they turn translucent. (They should still be crisp and tender to the bite.)
6. Transfer the onions to the peppers, arranging them in a single layer, and then lightly mix them in. Sprinkle with the oregano, parsley, salt, and pepper.

7. Pour the warm oil on top. Let the vegetables stand at room temperature for at least 1 hour before serving.
8. You also can put the vegetables in a tightly covered jar in the refrigerator and keep them for about a week. Bring them to room temperature before serving.

Yield: approximately 2 cups

Baked Stuffed Peppers

IIIIIIII

Serve with lasagne or manicotti, chicken or turkey. They also make a delicious sandwich the next day with any white poultry meat.

> *6 green Italian finger peppers*
> *1 cup fresh soft bread crumbs**
> *2 garlic cloves, chopped*
> *1 tablespoon chopped fresh parsley*
> *¼ cup freshly grated Parmesan cheese*
> *salt and pepper to taste*
> *olive oil*

1. Remove the stems and seeds from the peppers, leaving a small opening.
2. Mix together the bread crumbs, garlic, parsley, cheese, salt, and pepper. Drizzle olive oil over the mixture until it is well coated.
3. Push the bread stuffing into the pepper cavity.
4. Place the peppers on a baking sheet. Drizzle with more olive oil and sprinkle with salt.
5. Bake in a preheated 450-degree oven (use the middle rack) for about 20 minutes or until nicely browned.
6. Let the peppers rest ½ hour before transferring them to a serving platter. They will keep 2 or 3 days in the refrigerator.

   *NOTE: Use day-old Italian bread cut into small pieces and ground in a blender. Make coarse crumbs for stuffings and fine crumbs for coatings. They can be frozen in a plastic bag. Fresh or frozen-fresh bread crumbs make all the difference in the world to a recipe.

Serves 2–3

Baked Stuffed Peppers Sicilian Style

IIIIIII

This is a glorified stuffed pepper recipe. The peppers are standard for the holidays and very delicious. Serve them cold or hot with a sprinkle of tomato sauce, as desired.

> *4 large green peppers*
> *3 cups fresh bread crumbs (use French or Italian bread)*
> *2 garlic cloves, finely chopped*
> *1 can flat anchovies, rinsed and chopped (reserve oil)*
> *6 tablespoons capers, rinsed in cold water and finely chopped*
> *8 Sicilian, black, dry-cured olives, pitted and finely chopped*
> *4 tablespoons finely chopped fresh Italian parsley*
> *¼ cup freshly grated Parmesan cheese*
> *salt and freshly ground black pepper*
> *olive oil*

1. Cut the peppers in half, lengthwise, and remove stems and seeds.
2. In a large bowl, combine the bread crumbs, garlic, anchovies, capers, olives, parsley, Parmesan, salt, and pepper. Drizzle olive oil over the mixture and toss until the crumbs are slightly moistened.
3. Spoon the stuffing into the pepper halves and arrange them in a single layer in an oiled baking dish. Dribble a few drops of olive oil combined with the reserved anchovy oil over the top of each pepper.
4. Bake in the middle of a preheated 400-degree oven for about 30 minutes, or until the peppers are tender, but not limp, and the stuffing is light brown on top.

Serves 8

Zucchini Stew

IIIIIIII

⅓ cup olive oil
½ pound ground beef
1 small onion, chopped
2 cloves garlic, chopped
1 small green pepper, chopped
2 stalks of celery, chopped fine
*2 pounds small zucchini, washed and cut into
    ¼-inch rounds*
2 medium-size potatoes, cut into thin slices
*¾ cup canned tomatoes OR 1 tablespoon tomato
    paste*
salt, pepper, and red pepper flakes to taste
Parmesan cheese (reserve)

1. Using a large skillet, heat the olive oil. Saute the ground beef, onion, and garlic in the oil until browned.
2. Transfer the beef into a large soup pot and add the remaining ingredients (except the cheese) with 1½ cups of water.
3. Cover the pot and cook over medium-low heat for 30 minutes or until the zucchini is tender. Be sure not to overcook the zucchini. Serve in soup bowls and toss with Parmesan cheese if desired.

Serves 4

Zucchini Frittata

IIIIIIII

Zucchini Omelette

8 eggs
½ teaspoon salt
black pepper
¼ cup Parmesan cheese
2 medium zucchini, sliced thin
2 tablespoons chopped fresh parsley
2 tablespoons chopped fresh basil
1 tablespoon olive or salad oil

1. Beat the eggs with the salt and pepper. Stir in cheese, zucchini, parsley, and basil.
2. Preheat the broiler.
3. In a 10½-inch skillet, heat the oil. Add the eggs and cook undisturbed over low heat about 10 minutes. Carefully lift the edge to check the bottom — it should be golden brown.
4. Place the skillet under the broiler for 30 seconds until top is golden. Cut into wedges. Serve hot or at room temperature.

Serves 4

Batter-Fried Zucchini Sticks

IIIIIII

Many popular new restaurants are featuring this dish on their menus.

> *3 6-inch-long zucchini*
> *½ cup semolina or all-purpose flour*
> *2 teaspoons cornstarch*
> *1 large egg*
> *½ cup ice water*
> *olive oil for deep frying*
> *salt*
> *dried oregano*

1. Wipe the zucchini with a paper towel. Do not peel. Cut off the ends and discard. Cut the zucchini lengthwise into ¼-inch-thick strips, similar to carrot sticks.
2. In a medium-size bowl, stir together the flour and cornstarch.
3. In a small bowl, beat the egg until foamy. Add the water and beat to blend. Add the egg mixture to the flour mixture and stir just until moistened. The batter will be lumpy, but do not stir it again.
4. Pour olive oil into a skillet until it is about 2 inches deep. Heat the oil. Dip the zucchini sticks into the bat-

ter and place them, uncrowded, in the hot oil. When they have nicely browned on one side, turn them over to brown the second side.

5. When the sticks are golden brown on both sides, transfer them to paper toweling to drain. Sprinkle with salt and oregano. Serve hot as an appetizer or as a side dish.

Serves 4–6

Baked Zucchini with Anchovies and Tomatoes

IIIIIIII

This is very good when you are having a party or entertaining special company.

> 2 large zucchini (about 8–10 inches long)
> 3 small tomatoes
> 1 garlic clove, finely chopped
> 1 anchovy fillet in olive oil, crumbled
> 3 tablespoons olive oil
> pinch of dried oregano and basil, crushed
> 1 tablespoon fresh bread crumbs

1. Wash the zucchini and cut off and discard the tips. Slice the zucchini into 1/2-inch rounds.
2. Cook in boiling water for 5 minutes. Drain and let cool.
3. Meanwhile, slice the tomatoes crosswise into 1/2-inch slices. Let them drain on a platter for 30 minutes. Reserve the juices.
4. Layer the zucchini and tomato slices in an oiled baking pan. Combine the garlic, anchovy fillet, and olive oil, and pour onto the zucchini and tomatoes. Sprinkle with crushed oregano and basil and bread crumbs that have been moistened with the reserved tomato juices.
5. Bake in a preheated 375-degree oven for 25 minutes. Serve at room temperature. Cut in wedges and serve. This is also good as an appetizer.

Serves 4

Baked Zucchini Casserole

IIIIIIII

This is another delicious appetizer or party dish. It can be assembled ahead of time and baked just before serving.

> *6 small or 2 large firm zucchini*
> *2 eggs, beaten*
> *¼ cup fresh bread crumbs*
> *1 small onion, grated*
> *salt and freshly ground black pepper to taste*
> *4 tablespoons butter or margarine, melted*
> *¼ cup freshly grated Parmesan or Romano cheese*

1. Wash zucchini, cut off tips, and slice in ¼-inch rounds. Cook in a small amount of salted water until soft. Drain well and mash coarsely.
2. In a large bowl, combine the beaten eggs, bread crumbs, grated onion, salt, and pepper. Mix well. Toss with the melted butter until the crumbs are coated. Add the zucchini and mix gently.
3. Transfer the mixture to a baking dish. Sprinkle with the cheese. Bake in a preheated 350-degree oven for 30 minutes.
4. Serve at room temperature.

Serves 6

Fried Zucchini Blossoms

IIIIIIII

If you want to impress your friends with something exotic, here is the recipe for you. And the best part is that the preparation is simple. Your biggest challenge will be finding zucchini blossoms. These are the flowers that grow on a zucchini plant, so find someone who grows zucchini and you'll be all set.

> *24 zucchini blossoms*
> *1³/₄ cups flour*
> *pinch of salt*
> *3 teaspoons baking soda*
> *2 eggs, slightly beaten*
> *³/₄ cup milk*
> *¹/₄ cup water*
> *6 cups vegetable oil*

1. Do not wash the flowers. Clean by carefully removing the pistils.
2. Combine the flour, salt, baking soda, eggs, milk, and water. Stir until a smooth batter is obtained.
3. In a heavy frying pan, heat the oil to boiling. dip each flower into the batter, then put into the oil. Fry the flowers until they are golden brown on both sides. Remove with a slotted spoon and drain on paper toweling.
4. Sprinkle with salt and serve hot. They are best when served immediately.

Serves 4

Eggplant Parmigiana with Meat Sauce

IIIIIIII

This dish is a favorite in every Italian restaurant—and household! It is also very adaptable. It can be served with pasta or in sandwiches. Once you get the hang of it, its preparation will become quite simple.

> *2 small, dark, firm eggplants*
> *1½ cups oil, or more as needed*
> *flour*
> *4 eggs, beaten*
> *1 recipe Quick Meat Sauce (page 33)*
> *¾ cup mozzarella cheese, sliced or grated (optional)*
> *1 cup freshly grated Parmesan or Romano cheese*
> *chopped fresh parsley for garnish*

1. Remove the stem from each eggplant. Cut the eggplants crosswise into slices about ¼ inch thick. Do not remove the skin as this helps to hold the eggplant together.
2. Heat the oil in an electric frying plan on the highest heat, or use a large skillet.
3. Dust each eggplant slice with flour, dip into the beaten eggs, and fry on both sides until golden brown. (I like to use tongs to handle the eggplant.) Use more oil as needed. Drain on paper toweling. (If you prefer a thicker coating, you may dip the slices into coarse bread crumbs after dipping them into the egg wash.)
4. Line a 2½-quart shallow baking dish with a little of the meat sauce. Arrange a layer of eggplant slices over it. Cover with a layer of mozzarella cheese, more sauce, and a sprinkling of grated Parmesan cheese. Repeat the layers to use all ingredients. Pour leftover egg, if any, around the edges of the eggplant.
5. Bake in a preheated 350-degree oven for 30 minutes or until the eggplant is tender and golden on top.
6. Garnish with chopped parsley and serve.
7. For best results, let eggplant rest for 15 to 20 minutes before you cut it.

Caponata

||||||||

Pickled Eggplant

We usually serve this during Lent (*Pasqua*) or on Christmas Eve.

1 medium eggplant
¹/₃ cup olive or vegetable oil
1 medium onion, chopped
¹/₃ cup chopped green bell pepper
2 garlic cloves, crushed
1 4¹/₂-ounce jar whole mushrooms, drained,
    reserve liquid
1 6-ounce can tomato paste
¹/₂ cup pimiento-stuffed green olives
¹/₄ cup water and/or mushroom liquid
2 tablespoons red wine vinegar
1¹/₂ teaspoons sugar
¹/₂ teaspoon dried oregano, crushed
1 teaspoon salt
1/8 teaspoon pepper
1 handful of unsalted capers
2 small, whole, red chili peppers (optional)
1 or 2 bay leaves

1. Pare and dice the eggplant. You will need about 2 cups.
2. Heat the oil in a large heavy skillet. Saute the onion, pepper, and garlic for 2 minutes. Add the eggplant and mushrooms. Toss to mix well, cover, and simmer over very low heat for 10 minutes, stirring once.
3. Stir in the remaining ingredients. Cover and simmer, stirring once, until the eggplant is tender, about 15 minutes.
4. Cool to room temperature. Refrigerate overnight. Serve cold or warm.

Serves 4–8

Broccoli and Cauliflower Frittata

||||||||

Vegetables Fried in an Egg Batter

This recipe makes a great appetizer or side dish.

> *¹/₂ medium-size head of broccoli*
> *¹/₂ medium-size head of cauliflower*
> *3 eggs*
> *salt and freshly ground black pepper*
> *1¹/₂ cups fine fresh bread crumbs*
> *¹/₂ cup freshly grated Parmesan cheese*
> *oil*
> *1 large garlic clove*
> *lemon wedges for garnish*

1. Wash and trim the broccoli and cauliflower. Cut them into flowerets. Blanch them separately in salted boiling water about 4 minutes or until tender. Drain well and cool.
2. Beat the eggs in a shallow bowl with salt and pepper.
3. Combine the bread crumbs and grated cheese in a pie plate or shallow dish.
4. Dip the flowerets in the eggs, shaking off the excess. Coat with the bread crumb mixture and shake off the excess. Reserve.
5. Pour oil into a large heavy skillet, to about 1 inch deep. Heat over medium heat. Add the garlic and saute until golden, about 1 minute. Discard the garlic.
6. Fry the breaded flowerets in batches. Turn them over as they cook, until they are golden brown on all sides, about 3 minutes. Adjust the heat as necessary to keep the oil sizzling.
7. Transfer the flowerets to a baking pan lined with paper towels to drain. Keep them warm in the oven at the lowest setting until all of them have been fried. Serve with lemon wedges.

Serves 4–6

Sauteed Broccoli di Rabe or Mustard Greens

||||||||

1 pound broccoli di rabe OR mustard greens,
  washed and trimmed
olive oil
6 cloves garlic, whole
red pepper flakes
1 1-pound can cannellini beans, with juice
salt
pepper

1. If using broccoli di rabe, trim tough stems and cut remaining stalks in half. If using mustard greens, pick only the young tender leaves. Do not use the yellow flowers. Wash well.
2. In a large skillet, put enough olive oil to cover the bottom of the pan. Add the garlic and red pepper flakes and saute until the garlic is slightly brown.
3. Add the greens. Using high heat, cover and let cook slowly until the greens are limp but tender. Remove to a platter.
4. In the remaining broth, heat the beans with the juice from the can. Pour over the greens. Season to taste.

Serves 4 (as a side dish)

Lima Beans Italian Style

||||||||

Serve these beans with any meat or fish dish. If you wish, you may refrigerate them for several days.

1 garlic clove, chopped
4 tablespoons olive oil
2/3 cup canned tomatoes
pinch of dried oregano, red pepper flakes, and
  mint
salt and freshly ground black pepper to taste
1 cup hot water

1 16-ounce package frozen lima beans
1 celery stalk, chopped
freshly grated Parmesan cheese

1. In a medium saucepan, saute the garlic in the olive oil.
2. Add the tomatoes and seasonings. Simmer for 5 minutes, stirring often.
3. Add the water and let the sauce come to a boil.
4. Add the beans and celery, stir well, and let boil gently for a minute or two. Taste and add more seasonings, if desired.
5. Cover and gently boil for about 30 minutes or until the beans are tender. (Do not overcook.)
6. Sprinkle with grated cheese and serve.

Serves 3–4

Verdura
▮▮▮▮▮▮▮
Greens

1 pound tender young dandelion greens
1 large baking potato
salt
1 clove garlic, minced
2–3 tablespoons extra-virgin olive oil
fresh black pepper
juice of ½ lemon or to taste
½ teaspoon sugar (optional)

1. Remove the stems from the dandelion greens. Wash the leaves. Cut the leaves into ¼-inch strips, cutting across the leaf.
2. Peel the potato and cut it into ½-inch cubes. Place the potato cubes in cold salted water, bring to a boil, reduce the heat, and gently simmer for 3 to 4 minutes, or until tender. Refresh the potatoes under cold water and drain.
3. Meanwhile, cook the dandelion greens in rapidly boiling salted water for 1 to 2 minutes, or until tender. Refresh under cold water and drain.
4. Mince the garlic. (The recipe can be prepared to this stage up to 12 hours before serving.)
5. Just before serving, heat the olive oil in a skillet over

medium heat. Add the garlic and cook for 10 seconds. Add the dandelion greens and potatoes. Add salt and pepper to taste.

6. Saute the vegetables for 2 minutes, or until thoroughly heated. Add lemon juice to taste. If the greens are still bitter, add a little sugar.

Serves 4

Escarole Sauteed with Garlic

||||||||

2 pounds escarole
3 tablespoons olive oil
½ cup chopped onions
1 tablespoon coarsely chopped garlic (about 2 large cloves)

1. Trim the escarole and wash it thoroughly.
2. Cook it in boiling salted water until tender (about 5 minutes). Drain and chop. Don't squeeze the escarole dry; just drain it well. You should have 2½ to 3 cups chopped escarole.
3. Heat the oil in a large frying pan over medium-low heat. When the oil is warm, add the onions and garlic and saute until soft. Do not brown.
4. Stir in the chopped escarole and continue to cook for 3 minutes, or until the flavors are well blended. Add salt if necessary.

Serves 4–6

Marinated Mushrooms and Green Beans

||||||||

This dish can be served as a side dish or over spinach or lettuce salad, tossed with croutons and grated cheese.

2 garlic cloves, chopped
¹/₄ teaspoon grated lemon peel
¹/₄ cup fresh lemon juice
³/₄ cup olive oil
1 tablespoon chopped fresh parsley
pinch of dried oregano
salt and pepper to taste
¹/₂ pound fresh green beans, tips snapped off
2 cups sliced fresh mushrooms
1 tablespoon sliced scallions

1. Combine the first seven ingredients and mix well. Set the dressing aside.
2. Steam the green beans until tender but not soft, then plunge them into cold water. Drain well.
3. Mix the beans with the mushrooms and scallions. Pour the dressing over the vegetables and let them marinate about 2 hours.

Serves 4–6

Baked Stuffed Mushrooms with Ricotta

|||||||

These mushrooms are an excellent appetizer or side dish for a meat meal.

10 large fresh mushrooms
¹/₄ cup fresh bread crumbs
2 garlic cloves, pressed
1 tablespoon chopped fresh parsley
2 medium eggs
¹/₂ cup ricotta cheese
2 tablespoons freshly grated Parmesan cheese
salt and freshly ground black pepper to taste
¹/₄ cup olive oil

1. Wipe the mushrooms with paper towels. Remove the stems and finely chop them. Mix the chopped mushrooms with the bread crumbs, garlic, parsley, eggs, ricotta, grated cheese, salt, and pepper.
2. Fill each mushroom cap with the stuffing. Place on a shallow ovenproof pan.
3. Drizzle olive oil over each mushroom. Bake on the highest rack in a preheated 350-degree oven for 20 minutes. Serve hot.

Serves 5

Marinated Mushrooms

IIIIIII

Serve these mushrooms as an appetizer or put them over a fresh garden salad.

3/4 pound small, white fresh mushrooms
4 tablespoons fresh lemon juice
1/2 teaspoon Dijon-style mustard
1/4 teaspoon salt
1/4 teaspoon freshly ground black pepper
1/2 teaspoon dried oregano
3/4 cup olive oil
1 garlic clove, halved

1. Wipe the mushrooms with paper towels. Trim the stems.
2. In a large bottle with a tight-fitting lid (a mayonnaise jar will do), combine the lemon juice, mustard, salt, and pepper.
3. Stir until the mustard is blended with the juice and the salt has dissolved. Add the oregano, olive oil, and garlic. Cover the bottle tightly and shake well.
4. Add the mushrooms, cover, and shake again. Marinate in the refrigerator for at least 4 hours, shaking occasionally.
5. Drain the mushrooms before serving. If you are serving them as an appetizer, put them in a small bowl and serve with toothpicks.

Serves 2–4

Asparagus Parmigiana

IIIIIII

This asparagus recipe is a delicious accompaniment to any veal recipe especially, or to any light lunch with garlic bread.

> *1 1/2 pounds fresh asparagus*
> *1/2 cup butter or margarine*
> *1/2 cup freshly grated Parmesan or Romano cheese*
> *1 teaspoon salt*
> *1/2 teaspoon freshly ground black pepper*

1. Grease a 1 1/2-quart casserole dish.
2. Break off the lower part of the asparagus stalks as far down as they will snap. Discard. Thoroughly wash the asparagus.
3. Stand the spears in the bottom of a double boiler or in a deep saucepan. Cover the lower half of the spears with water. Cook, covered, for 15 minutes or until tender.
4. Melt the butter or margarine in a small saucepan and pour into the casserole dish. Place the cooked asparagus in the casserole and sprinkle with a mixture of the grated cheese, salt, and pepper.
5. Bake at 450 degrees for 5 to 10 minutes, or until the cheese has melted. Serve hot.

Serves 6

Patty's Artichoke Bake

IIIIIII

> *2 small jars artichoke hearts, drained*
>   *(reserve oil)*
> *3 green scallions, chopped*
> *4 eggs, beaten*
> *1/2 pound sharp cheddar cheese, grated*
> *1/4 cup grated Romano cheese*
> *6 crushed Saltine crackers*
> *6 tablespoons chopped parsley*
> *dash of Tabasco*
> *salt and pepper to taste*

1. Chop the artichokes coarsely.
2. Fry the scallions in 2 teaspoons of the reserved artichoke oil.
3. Add the beaten eggs and the remaining ingredients.
4. Lightly oil an 8- or 9-inch Pyrex casserole dish. Add the artichoke mixture and bake in a preheated 325-degree oven for 30 to 40 minutes, or until completely firm but not dry.
5. Let cool and cut into squares. Serve as an appetizer or a side dish.

Serves 6–8

Carcioffi alla Romana

IIIIIII

Stuffed Artichokes

A must for the holidays!

> *4 medium-size artichokes*
> *1 cup fresh bread crumbs (use day-old Italian bread)*
> *2 tablespoons chopped fresh parsley*
> *1/3 cup freshly grated Parmesan cheese*
> *1 garlic clove, chopped*
> *salt and pepper to taste*
> *olive oil*
> *3 garlic cloves, halved*

To Prepare Artichokes

1. Soak the artichokes in cold water for a half hour to release dirt.
2. Cut off the stem of one artichoke with a sharp knife. Carefully cut straight across the top to remove the prickly tips. Stand the artichoke upside down and give it a firm whack to open the leaves slightly for stuffing. Repeat with the other artichokes.

To Prepare Stuffing

1. Mix together in a large bowl the bread crumbs, parsley, grated cheese, the chopped garlic clove, salt, and pepper. Add enough oil to slightly moisten the mixture. Toss the crumbs until they are well coated with oil. Fill each cavity of the artichokes (inside the leaves) with stuffing until well packed.
2. Put 1 cup water and 1 tablespoon of salt in a deep saucepan.
3. Add the artichokes and the 3 halved garlic cloves.
4. Drizzle the tops with olive oil. Cover and let the water come to a boil. Lower the heat, and let the artichokes simmer about 45 minutes or until tender.
5. Serve warm or at room temperature, not hot.

    NOTE: To eat the artichokes, scrape off pulpy ends between the teeth.

Serves 4

Joanne's Spicy White Rice
IIIIIII

> olive oil
> 1 large soft green tomato, chopped
> 1 large ripe red tomato, chopped
> 1 small onion, chopped
> 1 clove garlic, chopped
> salt and pepper to taste
> 1 cup converted rice, washed and picked over

1. Using a medium-size saucepan, add enough olive oil to just cover the bottom of the pan.
2. Using medium heat, saute the chopped vegetables until tender. Add salt and pepper to taste and 2½ cups water. Cover.
3. When the water comes to a boil, add the rice. Stir well and cover.

4. Let simmer for 15 minutes and then shut the heat off. Push the pan to the back of the stove and let it set until the rice is fluffy.

NOTE: To serve 10–12: Use 5 cups water, 2 teaspoons salt; then add 2 cups rice.

Serves 6–8

Leek Patties

These patties are a good accompaniment to fish or meat.

> *4 leeks, trimmed and thinly sliced*
> *4 slices white bread, cubed*
> *¼ cup milk*
> *1 egg*
> *salt and pepper to taste*
> *½ cup flour, preferably semolina*
> *1 onion, thickly sliced*
> *½ cup olive oil*

1. Cover the leeks in salted boiling water and cook until they are tender.
2. Meanwhile, soak the bread cubes in the milk.
3. Drain the leeks well. Mix them with the soaked bread (thoroughly squeezed), egg, salt, and pepper.
4. Roll into medium-size patties. Slightly flatten the patties with your hands and quickly coat both sides with flour. Place the patties on a large platter and reserve.
5. In a large heavy skillet, saute the sliced onion until transparent in the olive oil. (Do not burn.)
6. Discard the onion and gently fry the patties on both sides until golden brown. Transfer to paper towels to drain before serving.

Yield: 6–8 patties

La Giambotta

IIIIIIII

Italian Vegetable Stew

When I was a child, my mother always had some kind of vegetable dish cooking on the stove. If she had any leftovers from it, she would beat a couple of eggs with grated cheese and toss the leftovers into the hot frying pan. After tossing the mixture just enough to cook the eggs, she would serve this for lunch sprinkled with hot pepper flakes. Scrumptious!

> *1 garlic clove, chopped*
> *1 large onion, chopped*
> *1/2 cup olive oil*
> *1 8-ounce can whole tomatoes*
> *salt and freshly ground black pepper to taste*
> *pinch of dried oregano, red pepper flakes, basil,*
>   *and mint*
> *1/2 cup hot water*
> *1 pound zucchini, cubed*
> *2 medium potatoes, peeled and cubed*
> *1 green bell pepper, thickly sliced*
> *2 celery stalks, sliced*
> *1 pound string beans, trimmed and cut in 1-inch*
>   *pieces*

1. In a large heavy skillet, saute the garlic and onion in the olive oil for 3 minutes.
2. Add the tomatoes, mashing them slightly with a large fork. Stir well, and add salt, pepper, and a sprinkle of seasonings. Saute for 5 minutes until well blended.
3. Add the hot water and stir well. Let the sauce come to a gentle boil.

4. Add the zucchini, potatoes, green pepper, celery, beans, and additional seasonings to taste. Let the mixture come to a gentle boil, cover, and simmer until the vegetables are tender, but not mushy.
5. Shut off the heat and let the stew rest for about 5 minutes for better flavor. Serve it in bowls, accompanied by crusty garlic bread and salad.

Serves 3–4

Pastries, Cookies, and Desserts

||||||||

Cannoli

||||||||

Making cannoli is rather time consuming, but they make a lovely and elegant presentation at any special function or festive occasion. The light and delicate crust and the heavy and creamy ricotta make a dessert that is hard to equal. To make cannoli, you must purchase at least 16 aluminum cannoli tubes, which are available at any specialty shop. All the ingredients need to be at room temperature.

Cannoli Shells

1³/₄ cups unsifted, all-purpose flour
¹/₂ teaspoon salt
2 tablespoons sugar
1 egg, slightly beaten
2 tablespoons firm butter, cut in small pieces
¹/₄ cup dry sauterne wine
1 egg white, slightly beaten
1 3-pound can solid vegetable shortening for
  frying

1. Sift the flour with the salt and sugar.
2. Make a well in the center and place the egg and butter in it. Stir with a fork, working from the center out, to moisten the flour mixture.
3. Add the wine, 1 tablespoon at a time, until the dough begins to cling together. Use your hands to form the dough into a ball. Cover and let stand for 15 minutes.
4. Roll part of the dough out on a floured board or a flat, smooth surface to at least ¹/₁₆ inch thick. Cut it into 3¹/₂-inch-long ovals (I cut a cardboard pattern to use as a guideline).
5. Loosely wrap an oval of dough around a cannoli tube, pinching the middle edges and sealing with beaten egg white. (Use your fingertips.) Turn out the ends of the dough to flare slightly. Prepare as many cannoli as you have tubes.

6. Meanwhile, heat the shortening in a large heavy pan, one that is deep enough for the shells to drop to the bottom and float to the top, uncrowded.
7. Using soft-edged tongs, deep-fry 2 or 3 cannoli at a time in the hot fat for about 1 minute or until golden brown.
8. Remove with tongs and drain on paper towels; let cool about 5 seconds, then slip out the cannoli tube, holding the shell carefully. (I usually very gently tap the tube edges on both sides, and then slip it out with no effort or breakage.) Repeat the process until all the dough is used. Add more fat as needed.
9. Cool before filling. They will be ready to fill as soon as you have finished cooking all the shells. Or they may be stored in a covered container and kept up to a month. Do not fill them until they are needed.

Ricotta Cannoli Filling

2 pounds (4 cups) chilled ricotta cheese
1 1/2 cups unsifted confectioners' sugar
4 teaspoons vanilla
1/2 cup finely chopped citron
1/2 cup finely chopped fresh orange peel
1/4 cup chopped sweet chocolate (optional)

1. Using the back of a large spoon, press the ricotta through a large wire strainer into a medium-size bowl. This will give a light, fluffy, and yet firm texture to the ricotta.
2. Blend in the remaining ingredients. Chill for 1 to 2 hours.

   VARIATION: To make a fluffy filling, prepare half of the above ricotta filling. Fold in 1 cup heavy cream, beaten until stiff. Chill for 1 to 2 hours.

To Finish Preparation

confectioners' sugar
chopped pistachio nuts or nut meats tinted with
  green food coloring

1. No more than 1 hour before serving, use a pastry tube or a long-handled, thin spoon to fill the cannoli shells. Do not overstuff. Keep refrigerated until serving time.
2. Sift confectioners' sugar over the shell. Garnish the ends with the chopped nuts.

Yield: 25 cannoli

Ricotta Cream Puffs
IIIIIIII

These are a lovely dessert and are easier to prepare than you may think. They also are very convenient to make for company, as the cream puffs may be baked early in the day and filled a couple of hours before serving.

Cream Puffs

½ cup solid vegetable shortening
⅛ teaspoon salt
1 cup boiling water
1 cup sifted flour
3 eggs

1. Add the shortening and salt to the cup of boiling water and stir over medium heat until the mixture resumes boiling.
2. Lower the heat. Add the flour all at once and stir vigorously until the mixture leaves the sides of the pan.
3. Remove the pan from the heat. Add the eggs, one at a time, beating thoroughly after each addition.
4. Shape on an ungreased cookie sheet, using a tablespoon of batter for each cream puff. You may use a pastry bag if you wish.
5. Bake in a preheated 450-degree oven for about 20 minutes. Then reduce the temperature to 350 degrees and bake for 20 minutes longer.
6. Remove the cream puffs from the oven and place on a rack to cool.

Ricotta Filling

¹/₄ cup confectioners' sugar
¹/₄ teaspoon grated lemon or orange rind
1 teaspoon vanilla extract
1 pound ricotta, well chilled

Add the confectioners' sugar, lemon or orange rind, and vanilla to the ricotta. Blend. Do not stir too long; just use quick strokes to mix all the ingredients or the ricotta will become too soft and milky and seep through the puffs.

To Finish Preparation

1. Cut the tops off the cooled cream puffs. Save the tops.
2. Fill the puffs with the filling. Replace the tops and dust with sifted confectioners' sugar. Refrigerate up to 2 hours before serving.

Yield: approximately 2¹/₂ dozen

Ricotta Cake

▌▌▌▌▌▌▌

This is a light, pielike treat. It can be made a day or two before serving and kept refrigerated.

3 pounds ricotta cheese
2 cups sugar
8 eggs, separated
¹/₂ cup sifted flour
grated rind of 1 lemon
1 teaspoon vanilla extract
¹/₂ cup cream, whipped
graham cracker crumbs (enough to coat pan)*

1. In a large bowl, using a wire whisk, beat the ricotta until smooth. Gradually add 1¹/₂ cups of the sugar and the egg yolks, beating after each addition. Beat in the flour, lemon rind, and vanilla.

2. In another bowl, beat the 8 egg whites with the remaining ½ cup sugar.
3. Gently fold the whipped cream and the beaten egg whites into the ricotta mixture.
4. Turn the batter into a 12-inch springform pan that has been well buttered and sprinkled with graham cracker crumbs.
5. Bake in a preheated 425-degree oven for 10 minutes. Lower the temperature to 350 degrees and continue baking for 1 hour.
6. Turn off the heat and allow the cake to cook in the oven with the door closed.
7. Refrigerate the cake until serving time. Top it with crushed sugared strawberries or cherries before serving.

   *NOTE: *Pasta frolla* (a crust of butter and sugar combined with flour), the crust for *Pizza Rustica*, or your favorite pie crust recipe may be used instead of a graham cracker crust.

Serves 12

Pizza Rustica

IIIIIIII

Deep-Dish Ricotta Pie

This is a truly excellent dessert. It is nice to serve at a party because it makes enough pieces to serve a large group.

Pastry

2 cups sifted flour
¾ teaspoon salt
⅔ cup solid vegetable shortening
1 egg
6–8 tablespoons cold water

1. Sift the flour with the salt into a large mixing bowl. Cut in the shortening until the mixture resembles cornmeal.

2. Add the egg and water. Blend together with quick motions.
3. Roll out the dough in a large rectangle to fit a glass or metal baking dish about 12 inches long, 8 inches wide, and 2 inches deep. Press it into the baking dish. Set aside while you prepare the filling.

Ricotta Pie Filling

2 pounds ricotta cheese
1 1/2 cups sugar
1/2 teaspoon salt
4 eggs, separated
2 teaspoons vanilla extract
1 cup milk
confectioners' sugar

1. Put the ricotta, sugar, salt, egg yolks, vanilla, and milk in a large bowl. Using a wooden spoon, blend until smooth.
2. Beat egg whites just until foamy, but not stiff. Gently fold into the ricotta mixture. Carefully pour the filling into the pastry shell.
3. Bake the pie in a preheated 400-degree oven for 20 minutes. Reduce the heat to 375 degrees and bake 45 minutes longer. Remove from the oven and cool.
4. Cut into wedges and serve cold or at room temperature. Refrigerate if holding several hours. Sprinkle with confectioners' sugar before serving.

Yield: approximately 20 pieces

Sweetened Ricotta with Fresh Fruit and Mint

IIIIIIII

Prepare about 40 minutes before serving.

1 pound ricotta
1/4 cup confectioners' sugar

2 medium-size oranges
1 pound seedless red or green grapes
mint leaves for garnish

1. In a large bowl, with mixer at low speed, beat the ricotta and confectioners' sugar until smooth.
2. Peel and section the oranges. Remove the grapes from stem, reserving 6 small clusters for garnish.
3. With a spatula, gently fold the orange sections and grapes into the ricotta mixture.
4. Spoon the fruit and ricotta mixture into six dessert bowls. Garnish with the grape clusters and mint leaves and refrigerate until ready to serve.

Serves 6

Tortoni

IIIIIIII

6 egg yolks
pinch of salt
3 tablespoons warm water
³/₄ cup sugar
¹/₄ cup water
1 tablespoon vanilla extract
3 tablespoons sherry
1 pint heavy cream
¹/₂ cup chopped almonds

1. Combine the egg yolks, salt, and warm water in the top of a double boiler. Over boiling water, beat until the yolks are light and lemon colored. Set aside.
2. Boil the sugar and ¹/₄ cup water over medium heat, stirring constantly, until the syrup spins a thread from the end of a spoon.
3. Cool the syrup slightly, then beat it into the egg yolks, beating rapidly and constantly. Cook over hot, not boiling, water, stirring constantly, until thick, about 8 minutes. Remove from heat and cool to room temperature.
4. Add the vanilla and sherry and let the mixture cool some more.

5. Beat the cream until it is thick but not stiff. Stir the cream into the custard. Pour into 12 fluted paper cups.
6. Sprinkle the tops with the chopped almonds. Put the cups in the freezer.
7. Freeze until firm, about 3 hours, or for a few days. If desired, tortoni may be frozen in ice cube trays and served in sherbet glasses.

Serves 12

Biscotti

IIIIIIII

Biscotti are dry, plain cookies that are enhanced by the flavor of anise. They are excellent with a cup of coffee in the morning or midafternoon when you only want a little something to eat.

> *3 well-beaten eggs*
> *1 cup sugar*
> *¹/₂ cup margarine, melted*
> *2 teaspoons vanilla extract*
> *1 tablespoon anise extract*
> *1 cup chopped walnuts (optional)*
> *2 cups flour*
> *2 teaspoons baking powder*
> *¹/₂ teaspoon salt*

1. Combine the first six ingredients in a large mixing bowl.
2. Sift together the flour, baking powder, and salt.
3. Fold the dry ingredients into the egg mixture and beat until smooth and satiny. If the dough is too soft to handle, add more flour as needed.
4. Roll the dough into little loaves: 2 or 3 loaves if you wish large cookies, 4 loaves for smaller ones. Place these loaves on an ungreased cookie sheet.
5. Bake in a preheated 375-degree oven until brown, about 25 minutes. Remove from the oven and cool.
6. When cool, slice the loaves diagonally into ¹/₂-inch slices. Arrange the slices on the ungreased baking sheet

and return to a 350-degree oven to dry out and toast until light golden.

7. Cool, then put in a covered container. They will keep indefinitely.

Yield: approximately 2 dozen

Nancy's Nutty Biscotti
▌▌▌▌▌▌▌

Have all the ingredients at room temperature before you begin preparation.

> *1 1/2 cups sugar*
> *1/2 pound margarine*
> *2 eggs*
> *1 1/2 cups milk*
> *2 teaspoons vanilla extract*
> *2 teaspoons cinnamon*
> *3 cups unbleached flour (King Arthur preferred)*
> *1 teaspoon baking soda*
> *2 teaspoons baking powder*
> *1/2 cup walnuts*
> *1/2 cup crushed almonds (optional)*
> *1 cup chocolate morsels (semisweet or milk chocolate)*

1. Using a large bowl, cream together the sugar and margarine. Add the eggs, milk, vanilla, and cinnamon. Mix well. Add 1 cup of the flour, baking soda, and baking powder. Mix well again.
2. Add the nuts and chocolate morsels. Add the remaining flour and stir well until you form a firm dough. If the dough is too soft, add more flour.
3. Form 3 loaves on ungreased cookie sheets. If you wish to make small cookies, form the loaves in a long rope shape. For large cookies, keep the dough short and wide. Keep the loaves well spaced to allow the dough to spread.
4. Bake in a preheated 350-degree oven for 20 minutes until dark brown in color. Test with a toothpick for doneness.
5. Take out of oven and cool on a rack. Cut in slices to form biscotti. Store in a covered container for up to two weeks.

Yield: 30-36

Biscuit Tortoni

IIIIIIII

*¹/₂ cup crushed Italian macaroons (without
  almonds)*
¹/₂ cup crushed toasted almonds
¹/₄ cup confectioners' sugar
2 cups heavy cream
3 tablespoons rum
6 maraschino cherries for garnish

1. Mix together the crushed macaroons, three-fourths of
   the almonds, confectioners' sugar, and 1 cup of the
   cream.
2. Whip the second cup of cream until it is stiff. Fold it
   into the macaroon mixture, alternating with the rum.
3. Spoon into small paper cups and freeze. After 2 hours,
   sprinkle the tops with the remaining crushed almonds.
   Place a maraschino cherry in the center of each cup.
   Return the desserts to the freezer until serving time.

Serves 6

Zabaglione

IIIIIIII

4 egg yolks
4 tablespoons sugar
³/₄ cup port or Marsala wine
pinch of cinnamon

1. Beat the yolks until they are light and lemon colored.
   Gradually add the sugar, beating constantly. Add the
   wine and beat well.

2. Pour into the top of a double boiler and cook over hot, not boiling, water until thick, beating constantly with a rotary beater.
3. Pour into dessert dishes, sprinkle with cinnamon, and serve. Or chill and serve as a sauce over fruit.

Serves 6

Brandied Cherries

These cherries must be stored for a month before using. This can be helpful if you are making them for a holiday when you will be busy with other things.

> *2 pounds Bing cherries*
> *2 cups brandy*
> *2 cups sugar*
> *1 cup water*

1. Wash the cherries and cut off half of each stem.
2. Place the cherries in two sterilized quart jars and cover them with the brandy. Cover the jars, but do not seal. Let stand overnight.
3. Boil the sugar and water together for 10 minutes. Skim the surface and cool.
4. Drain the brandy from the cherries and add it to the syrup. Stir well. Pour the liquid back into the jars over the cherries. Seal tightly. Store in a cool, dark cupboard.

Yield: 2 quarts

Brandied Chestnuts

Chestnuts must be blanched and shelled before they can be used. There are many ways to blanch them. This is an easy one: Cut slits in each nut before putting them in a pan covered with water. Boil gently until tender, about 30 minutes. Drain, then remove shells and skins. Chestnuts prepared this way are easily pureed or mashed. Brandied chestnuts must be stored for a month before using them.

> 1 ¼ cups sugar
> 1 cup water
> 1 pound chestnuts, blanched and shelled
> 1 cup brandy

1. Boil the sugar and water together in a small saucepan for 10 minutes. Skim the surface.
2. Put the peeled chestnuts in a bowl, and pour the hot syrup over them. Cover and let stand overnight.
3. The next day, drain the syrup from the chestnuts and combine with the brandy in a saucepan. Bring to a boil.
4. Put the chestnuts in a hot, sterilized quart jar or two pint jars, and pour boiling syrup over them. Seal tightly. Store in a cool, dark cupboard.

Yield: 1 quart

Torta di Castagne

IIIIIIII

Chestnut Torte

Follow the blanching and shelling instructions for chestnuts given in the recipe for Brandied Chestnuts. Then puree the chestnuts in a blender or food processor.

> 1 cup cake flour
> 1 teaspoon baking powder
> 6 tablespoons butter
> ⅔ cup sugar
> 1 pound chestnuts, pureed
> 1 teaspoon vanilla extract
> 6 eggs, separated

1. Sift the cake flour, measure, and resift with the baking powder three times. Set aside.
2. Cream the butter and sugar. Add the chestnut puree and vanilla and beat well. Add the egg yolks one at a time, beating well after each addition.
3. In another bowl, beat the egg whites until they hold a soft peak. Fold into the chestnut mixture. Then fold the sifted dry ingredients into the mixture.
4. Line a greased 9x13-inch pan with waxed paper. Pour in the batter. Bake in a preheated 350-degree oven for 40 minutes, or until the torte shrinks from the sides of the pan.
5. Cool in the pan for 5 minutes, then turn out onto a cake rack and remove the waxed paper.
6. This will keep very well if it is wrapped in waxed paper and stored in a cool place. Before serving, sprinkle the top with confectioners' sugar, if you wish.

Serves 8–10

Savoiardi

▌▌▌▌▌▌▌

Lady Fingers

I like to serve these with a cup of coffee or use them in any recipe calling for lady fingers.

> *4 eggs, separated*
> *¹/₈ teaspoon salt*
> *10 tablespoons sugar*
> *2 teaspoons vanilla extract*
> *¹/₃ cup sifted flour*

1. Cut a brown paper bag to line two cookie sheets.
2. Beat the egg whites and salt until foamy. Add 2 tablespoons of the sugar, and beat until soft peaks form. Set aside.

3. In another bowl, beat the egg yolks until thickened. Then gradually beat in the remaining sugar and the vanilla. Beat until very thick and lemon colored.
4. Sprinkle the flour over the egg yolk mixture. Then fold in the flour carefully. Now fold the egg yolk mixture into the egg whites.
5. Using a pastry tube or spoon, make 3-inch-long finger shapes of batter 2 inches apart on the brown paper.
6. Bake in a preheated 350-degree oven for 5 minutes, or until deep golden brown. Cool 2 to 3 minutes.
7. With a sharp knife, carefully remove the lady fingers from the paper. Store in an airtight container when dry and cool.

Yield: 3 dozen

Vincenzo's Zucchini Bread

Vincent was a former employer of the North End Union and very interested in health food. His zucchini bread was so rich and moist, it was like eating a complete meal. It became one of our favorite recipes.

3 eggs
2¹/₄ cups sugar
2 cups shredded zucchini
1¹/₂ teaspoons vanilla extract
1 cup oil
3 cups flour
¹/₂ teaspoon baking powder
4 teaspoons cinnamon
1 teaspoon baking soda
1 teaspoon salt
1 cup chopped nuts

1. Mix the first five ingredients in a large bowl.
2. Mix the next five ingredients in a second bowl.
3. Mix the dry ingredients into the zucchini mixture. Add the chopped nuts.

4. Grease and flour two 9x5-inch loaf pans. Pour in the batter.
5. Bake at 350 degrees for 1 hour. (They may take a little longer, so test with a toothpick.) Cool and serve at room temperature.
   NOTE: This bread may be frozen.

Serves 14

Striscia di Vino

IIIIIIII

Wine Strips

Wine strips are an excellent, fancy Italian cookie. They are so crisp and light your guests will never stop eating them.

> *2 cups all-purpose flour*
> *¹/₂ teaspoon baking powder*
> *3 tablespoons sugar*
> *¹/₄ cup butter*
> *¹/₂ cup Italian red wine*
> *2 cups oil*
> *¹/₂ cup confectioners' sugar*
> *1 teaspoon cinnamon*

1. Sift the flour, measure, and resift with the baking powder and sugar.
2. Cut the butter into the flour with your fingers until the mixture resembles cornmeal. Make a well in the flour and pour the wine into it. Mix the wine into the flour. Knead the dough until smooth, about 5 minutes.
3. Wrap the dough in waxed paper and set aside for 2 hours. Do not chill.
4. Roll the dough into a rectangle, ¹/₄ inch thick. Cut it into strips 1 inch wide and 4 inches long.
5. In a deep heavy skillet or pan, heat the oil on medium-high heat.

6. Drop about 4 strips of dough at a time into the hot oil, and fry until they are golden brown. Turn them over as they rise to the surface (using a pair of tongs makes this easy).
7. Remove the strips from the oil with tongs or a slotted spoon and drain on absorbent paper. Repeat until all the strips are fried.
8. Combine the confectioners' sugar and cinnamon. Sprinkle it over the strips when they are cool. Arrange on a pretty platter and serve.

NOTE: These will keep in a covered container for a while. Put a piece of paper toweling in the bottom of the container to absorb any moisture. Do not sprinkle with confectioners' sugar until just before serving.

Yield: 2¹/₂ dozen

Zeppole

IIIIIII

Fried Dough

Anyone who has ever been to an Italian feast will recognize the enticing smell and taste of these fried treats. Once you master the recipe, you can experiment with shapes, like the outdoor vendors do. My grandmother used to stuff the dough with cauliflower, chopped anchovies, or codfish before cooking it. This was done by wrapping the dough around the cooked ingredient before dropping it into the hot oil.

> *1 3-pound can solid vegetable shortening for*
> *   frying*
> *2 eggs, beaten*
> *1¹/₂ cups milk*
> *2 cups unbleached flour, unsifted (King Arthur*
> *   preferred)*
> *1 teaspoon baking powder*
> *¹/₂ teaspoon salt*
> *confectioners' sugar*

1. Heat the shortening in a deep, wide fryer (a heavy-duty wok works well) until hot, but not burning. You will need the shortening to be about 6 inches deep.
2. In a large bowl, combine the eggs, milk, flour, baking powder, and salt. Using a large wooden spoon, mix thoroughly to form a smooth dough.
3. When the dough is pliable, drop it by heaping table-spoonfuls into the hot oil. Do only about 3 at the same time so that they do not touch each other or the sides of the pan. Fry until golden brown on all sides. Remove with a slotted spoon and drain on paper towels. The shortening may be cooled, strained, and stored to be used another time.
4. When cool, transfer to a large platter and sprinkle with confectioners' sugar. Serve as a snack or dessert. They are best served the day they are made.

Yield: 1 dozen

Cenci

IIIIIIII

Fried Bowknots

These are light and delicate, oddly shaped cookies. They are very interesting for an afternoon tea or a special lunch-eon dessert. Some people like to drizzle them with honey and sprinkle on multicolored candies for a colorful effect.

4 egg yolks
1 egg white
¹/₂ teaspoon salt
¹/₄ cup confectioners' sugar, plus more for dusting
1 teaspoon vanilla extract
1 teaspoon rum
1 cup flour
1 3-pound can solid vegetable shortening

1. Combine the egg yolks and egg white. Add the salt and beat 8–10 minutes on high speed with an electric mixer,

or use a wire whisk and beat rapidly.

2. Add the sugar and flavorings and beat until well blended, about 2 minutes. Add the flour a little at a time, lightly folding it in.

3. Transfer the dough to a well-floured surface and knead until the dough blisters, about 5 minutes. If no blisters form, and the dough seems quite smooth, cover it with a towel and let it rest for about 20 minutes.

4. Divide the dough into 4 parts. Roll out one part at a time on a lightly floured board to paper-thinness.

5. Cut into strips ½ inch wide and 6 inches long. Tie each strip into a loose bowknot or twist. Let dry for about 5 minutes or until the oil is ready.

6. Using a large, deep, and heavy pan, heat the shortening to 375 degrees. Fry the bowknots, uncrowded, until golden brown, turning once. Using a slotted spoon or tongs, carefully lift them out of the oil. Drain on paper towels. (The oil can be strained and stored for a future use.)

7. Transfer to a large serving platter and sprinkle with confectioners' sugar.

NOTE: These keep very well in a covered container, with a piece of paper toweling on the bottom of the container. Do not sprinkle with the sugar until just before serving.

Yield: 3–4 dozen

Carnevale Sfinge

IIIIIII

Light, Spongy Fritters

Carnevale Sfinge and *Zeppole* are typical desserts for any festive occasion, especially Carnival Night, the day before Lent. Years ago, Carnival Night was a big celebration, when cannoli or any ricotta dessert also were special favorites, but, alas, this tradition seems to be fading.

2 cups vegetable or peanut oil
1 1/2 cups flour
pinch of salt
3 teaspoons baking powder
1 1/4 cups sugar
2 small eggs
1/2 cup water
cinnamon (optional)

1. Heat the oil in a deep frying pan over medium-high heat until it is hot, but not burning.
2. Sift the flour, salt, baking powder, and 1/4 cup of the sugar together.
3. In a small bowl, whisk the eggs and water. Blend into the dry ingredients.
4. Dip a tablespoon into a glass of cold water and fill it with a heap of batter. (The water keeps the batter from sticking to the spoon.) Slide the batter into the hot oil (use a spatula to help get the batter out of the spoon). Fry 2 or 3 puffs at a time until golden brown (about 3 minutes).
5. Drain on paper towels. Roll in the remaining cup of sugar while still hot. (A sprinkle of cinnamon in the sugar can be very tasty also.) Serve immediately.

Yield: 10–12 puffs

Nancy's Lemon-Flavored Cookies

||||||||

These wonderful cookies are usually seen on special occasions, such as birthdays, anniversaries, and holidays, because the recipe makes a large amount. Anise, almond, or vanilla extract can be substituted for the lemon extract.

1 cup sugar
3/4 cup (12 heaping tablespoons) butter-flavored or regular shortening

6 eggs
¹/₂ cup milk
*5 cups unbleached flour, unsifted (King Arthur
    preferred)*
6 heaping teaspoons baking powder
*1¹/₂ tablespoons lemon extract, plus 1 teaspoon
    for the frosting*
1 pound confectioners' sugar
a little warm milk
multicolored candies or jimmies (optional)

1. In a large bowl, cream the sugar and shortening. Add the eggs, one at a time, mixing well after each addition.
2. Add the milk, flour, baking powder, and extract. Mix well. The dough will be soft. Add more flour if it is sticky.
3. Keep your hands well floured to smoothly handle the dough. Break off pieces to form 1-inch balls. Roll each ball between your hands to form a thin roll, like a pencil. Twist it into a mound to form a pyramid shape. Seal the ends or they will separate from the mound and spoil the shape. (The dough can also be twisted into the letter S or a figure eight. All these shapes are traditional.)
4. Bake in a preheated 400-degree oven on an ungreased cookie sheet for about 8 to 10 minutes or until the cookies are brown on the bottom, but light on top. Large cookies will require 10 to 15 minutes of cooking.
5. Remove from heat and cool.
6. Combine the confectioners' sugar with the remaining teaspoon of extract. Slowly add enough warm milk to make a thin frosting. Frost the cooled cookies.
7. Sprinkle the frosted cookies with multicolored candies or jimmies, if desired.

   NOTE: These cookies may be stored in plastic bags, with about 10 or 12 per bag.

Yield: 4 dozen small or 2 dozen large cookies

Anise Tea Cookies

IIIIIIII

This dough will be on the crumbly side while you're preparing it, but the net result will be a very lovely and delicate cookie.

> *2¹/₂ cups sifted all-purpose flour*
> *¹/₂ teaspoon salt*
> *¹/₄ cup chopped walnuts, pecans, or other nuts*
> *1 tablespoon anise seeds, or 1 teaspoon anise extract*
> *²/₃ cup vegetable oil*
> *²/₃ cup confectioners' sugar, plus more for dusting*
> *2 tablespoons orange juice*
> *1 teaspoon vanilla extract*

1. In a large mixing bowl combine the first five ingredients.
2. In a small bowl, combine the confectioners' sugar, orange juice, and vanilla. Then add this mixture to the mixture in the large bowl. Mix only until well blended. The dough will be rather crumbly and dry.
3. Take a piece of dough about the size of a walnut in your hand. With your fingers pressing into the palm of your hand, squeeze the middle of the dough to hold it together. Then pinch the ends in order to form a small crescent (half-moon) shape. Place the dough on a baking sheet and rearrange until it holds its crescent shape.
4. Bake the cookies at 350 degrees for 15 minutes (for smaller cookies) or 20–25 minutes (for larger cookies). They should be lightly browned when done.
5. Remove from the oven. Roll the warm cookies in additional confectioners' sugar. Cool, then store in a covered container. They will keep about 2 weeks.

Yield: 2–3 dozen

Ricotta Cookies

IIIIIII

These cookies are a nice surprise because they have the rich taste of butter, but the ricotta makes them light.

> $^1\!/_4$ *pound butter, at room temperature*
> $^1\!/_4$ *cup ricotta cheese*
> *1 teaspoon vanilla extract*
> *1 cup sugar*
> *1 egg*
> *2 cups sifted flour*
> $^1\!/_2$ *teaspoon baking soda*
> $^1\!/_2$ *teaspoon salt*

1. Blend the butter with the ricotta until creamy. Add the vanilla and mix well.
2. Gradually add the sugar, beating until well blended. Add the egg and mix well.
3. Slowly stir in the flour, baking soda, and salt, blending well.
4. Drop the batter from a teaspoon onto a greased baking sheet.
5. Bake in a preheated 350-degree oven for 10 minutes.
6. Cook, then transfer to a serving platter, using a spatula. They will keep for several weeks if stored in a covered container.

Yield: 36 cookies

Granita di Limone

IIIIIII

Lemon Ice

> *1 envelope unflavored gelatin*
> $^1\!/_4$ *cup cold water*
> *4 cups water*
> *1 cup sugar*

juice of 3 lemons
4 lemon slices for garnish

1. Soften the gelatin in the ¼ cup of cold water.
2. In a large saucepan, boil the 4 cups of water and sugar together for 5 minutes. Remove from the heat and add the lemon juice.
3. Add the softened gelatin to the syrup, stirring until dissolved.
4. Pour into a shallow pan and freeze until almost firm, about 2 or 3 hours. Transfer to the refrigerator 20 to 30 minutes before serving to allow the ice to soften a little. To serve, scoop into individual bowls and garnish with a slice of lemon.

Serves 4

Gelato

IIIIIIII

Italian Sherbet

2 cups water
2 cups sugar
pinch of salt
1 cup fresh lemon juice
grated rind of 1 lemon
2 egg whites

1. Boil water, sugar, and salt together for 5 minutes over medium heat.
2. Strain the lemon juice into the sugar syrup. Add the grated lemon rind. Cool.
3. Beat the egg whites until stiff but not dry. Fold them gently into the cooled syrup.
4. Pour into a shallow pan, cover with waxed paper, and freeze until firm, about 3 hours.

Serves 4

Index

▌▌▌▌▌▌▌